PENGUIN BUSINESS

BEING AN IMPACT CHAMPION

Priya Nair Rajeev is associate professor in Organizational Behavior and heads the Center of Excellence for Social Innovation, Indian Institute of Management Kozhikode (IIMK). She holds a PhD in management studies from IIT Madras and trained in participant-centered learning from Harvard Business School. A recipient of the Emerald/EFMD Outstanding Doctoral Research Award (2011), she is a gold medalist and university rank holder at the undergraduate, graduate, and postgraduate levels. She has been the chairperson of Executive Education programs, and of the Organizational Behavior and Human Resources area. She has to her credit several published articles in international journals and two co-authored books including *Indian Cases in Organisational Behaviour*. A prolific trainer, her areas of interest include managing emotions, leadership and personal growth, social innovation, and women in management.

Simy Joy, a PhD from Case Western Reserve University, USA and a fellow of Higher Education Academy, UK, has served as a faculty member at the University of East Anglia, UK and at IIM Kozhikode. She was a founding member of the Centre of Excellence for Social Innovation at IIMK. Her research interests include institutional and organizational sources of inequality, exclusion, and injustice; social innovations, social enterprises, socio-tech enterprises; and micro-enterprises that attempt to engender equality, inclusion, and justice. The winner of multiple international research awards, she has co-authored and co-edited books on social and socio-tech innovations.

Celebrating 35 Years of
Penguin Random House India

PRAISE FOR THE BOOK

'This book shows how young managers can indeed turn their corporate jobs into opportunities to address social and environmental issues that need addressing urgently and meaningfully. For those who wonder how they can take on these challenging issues, this book lays out three clear and actionable pathways—CSR, corporate social innovation, and social entrepreneurship—which they can choose from depending on their inclinations and circumstances. Written in a lucid and accessible style, using only Indian examples, it describes the pathways, key challenges, and most importantly, how to address them'—Nagaraja (Naga) Prakasam, Founder Chairman, Nativelead; Partner, Acumen Fund; lead angel investor and founding angel, IAN Impact

'The book boldly introduces the concept of Corporate Social Consciousness and sketches out the role of an Impact Champion to enact it—as an intrapreneur through CSR and CSI or outside an organization as a social entrepreneur'—Dr. Sapna Poti, Director, Strategic Alliances, Office of the Principal Scientific Adviser to the Government of India

'This book lays out a multi-level and multidimensional approach to impact assessment, an area critical for ensuring CSR projects' effectiveness'—Nixon Joseph, CEO, CLT India; CSR consultant; former President and Chief Operating Officer, SBI Foundation

Being an Impact Champion

Enacting Corporate Social Consciousness

Priya Nair Rajeev
and Simy Joy

Series Editor: Debashis Chatterjee

PENGUIN
BUSINESS

An imprint of Penguin Random House

PENGUIN BUSINESS

USA | Canada | UK | Ireland | Australia
New Zealand | India | South Africa | China | Singapore

Penguin Business is part of the Penguin Random House group of companies
whose addresses can be found at global.penguinrandomhouse.com

Published by Penguin Random House India Pvt. Ltd
4th Floor, Capital Tower 1, MG Road,
Gurugram 122 002, Haryana, India

Penguin
Random House
India

First published by SAGE Publications India Pvt. Ltd in 2022
Published in Penguin Business by Penguin Random House India 2023

ISBN 9780143461784

Typeset in Sabon by Manipal Technologies Limited, Manipal

www.penguin.co.in

To Papa,
for being the best father anyone could ask for.
Your belief in me, even during moments of doubt,
gave me the courage to pursue my passion.
Your love lives on in me.
—P.N.R.

To Sr Isaac, our primary school teacher, who made us
believe that being an Impact Champion is well within
the capabilities of eight-year-olds.
—S.J.

Contents

Part 3
Pathway 2—Social and Sustainable
Business Innovation

Part 4
Pathway 3—Social Entrepreneurship

Part 5
Embarking on the Journey

Preface

There is a growing interest and a sense of urgency the world over in finding ways of being socially conscious— to be benign in our engagement with Nature and with each other. Inspired individuals increasingly realize the need to be more actively involved in solving the many wicked problems surrounding us. Issues of poverty, inequality, disease, and a deteriorating environment with polluted air, increasing water scarcity, depleted soil, and freakish weather conditions remind us often enough that we have imperiled ourselves, and now we need to urgently course correct.

The genesis of this book was the Certificate Program in Social Initiatives, the first full-fledged course offered in social innovation by the Centre of Excellence for Social Innovation (CESI) at the Indian Institute of Management Kozhikode. The program got us thinking about the need for communicating ways in which inspired individuals could translate their social consciousness into action. This book reflects our quest to help an individual manager be convinced about the need to take on the challenge personally by being an Impact Champion. We lay a trail for social consciousness, traversing three pathways—corporate social responsibility, corporate social innovation, and social entrepreneurship.

Steering the organization to a path of social consciousness will require promoting greater introspection, reflection, and a course correction in our current ways of working and living. This is tough, as most of us are soaked in the idea that profitability imperatives and social consciousness are inherently disjunctive. So, while it is assumed that corporates should focus on profitability, enacting social consciousness has been handed over to the social sector.

We attempt to expose the absurdity of such assumptions, bring together these two worlds, and plant an idea of a socially conscious corporate. We hope this book will convey the urgency to change our ways and inspire managers to self-label themselves as Impact Champions who will lead that change.

Acting with social consciousness is our only escape from total annihilation. We must act, and soon enough!

Part 1

Being an Impact
Champion—An
Introduction

'The first step to becoming a changemaker is to give
oneself permission, i.e., to ignore—politely, of
course—all those who say "'Don't do it".'
—Bill Drayton, Social entrepreneurship
pioneer & Founder of Ashoka

1

Social Consciousness: The Imperative for Our Times

The month of March 2020 saw an unprecedented movement of labor within the country. The national lockdown announcement on the 24th to pre-empt the spread of the first wave of the Covid-19 pandemic confined 1.3 billion people within their homes. The lockdown brought industry and trade to a grinding halt for the next twenty-one days, followed by two more extensions till the 31st of May.

While the employed middle class could stay indoors in relative comfort, the unexpected lockdown imperiled migrant workers who had left their homes far behind, searching for a livelihood in other states of India. With only temporary sheds in the worksite as a shelter, meager savings, no social security net for succor, and an uncertain future, returning home to their villages seemed to be their only hope for survival. Instead, what stretched in the weeks that followed was a mass exodus of people walking thousands of miles with children, bundles of belongings, and perhaps a bottle of water. Several watched in horror the tragedy that trudged along the roads, covering unthinkable distances under the scorching sun with no means of transportation. The lockdown announced to pre-empt the pandemic had pushed the unsuspecting migrant workers onto the rugged roads of an unprepared nation. Civil society, followed by the government, took more than a month to arrange buses and trains.

A year later, migrant workers watched with trepidation as the second pandemic wave swept across India, ravaging several cities, including the national capital, reminded of how the last lockdown had left them jobless, with no means to get home. This time the Delhi High Court stepped in to warn the government to ensure that migrant workers were not put to any hardship and that buses and trains must continue to ply within and across states.

Reflecting on this avoidable tragedy can fill any right-thinking mind with guilt for having done little to intervene and indignation for allowing it to happen.

~

At first, what may appear to be an outlier event is irrefutable evidence of our failure on the economic and equity front. What else explains people being swiftly pushed into deprivation and desperation? Where have we failed that our brethren cannot survive a few days without work?

The plight of the migrant laborers is not a catastrophe that can be attributed solely to governmental failure. The 'market forces' that override ethical and human considerations have contributed their might to the gradual build-up of this reality over several decades. The unorganized workers amount to 53.8 crores (in a population of 139 crores) and work in agriculture, mining, construction, and service sectors. Though labor legislation mandates labor contractors to register with state governments and take appropriate licenses when they employ workers from other states, most of these rules are hardly ever implemented*. Contractors employing more than five migrant laborers are bound by law to provide proper wages, housing, medical facilities, pass-books, and even a displacement allowance, all missing when the migrant laborers needed them the most—during the lockdown. Our labor reforms have covered about 10 percent of the labor force who form the organized sector under their protection, leaving the disproportionately large unorganized industry exposed to market vagaries.

Nor can the corporates take cover from blame as they engage labor contractors to find and manage the workforce for the most arduous tasks, keeping them

---

* Jawhar Sircar, 'A Long Look at Exactly Why and How India Failed Its Migrant Workers', Wire, 29 May 2020, https://thewire.in/labour/lockdown-migrant-workers-policy-analysis.

out of 'expensive' direct employment. Subcontracting has, over the years, created a reality that allows companies to deny their responsibility towards laborers they employ, albeit indirectly.* Laborers who built our homes had to find shelter in their workplace—partially constructed apartments and office complexes, having been left homeless.

Our 'dystopic' existence

The plight of the migrant workers, hungry and dispossessed, are ominous signs of our society edging closer to a dystopian version. Firstly, governmental policies and actions often aggravate inequalities, exclusion, and societal polarizations than address them. The fundamental right of equality and non-discrimination has been violated in many instances. Equality of opportunity in public employment is threatened by poor economic growth and its consequent low job creation. Economic policies to promote market action tend to favor the prominent private sector players; their effects are yet to trickle down to the MSME sector. Finally, the stricter approaches that curtail the freedom of speech, expression, and opinion limit the opportunities to constructively partake in

---

* Chitra Rawat and Priyansha Singh, 'How Construction Industry Got Away With Not Paying Workers In Lockdown', BQ Prime, 3 June 2020, https://www.bqprime.com/economy-finance/how-construction-industry-got-away-with-not-paying-workers-in-lockdown.

policymaking in ways that cater to the interests of the wider society.

Secondly, our relationship with nature is deteriorating because of unchecked deforestation, urbanization, and our colossal failure to implement efficient waste management systems. Cities are overflowing with garbage, and sewage flows incessantly into the holiest of our rivers and seeps into the earth, contaminating our groundwater. The Covid-19 pandemic has created 33,000 tonnes of waste produced in just seven months, including PPE kits, masks, shoe covers, gloves, human tissues, items contaminated with blood, body fluids like dressings, plaster casts, cotton swabs, beddings, blood bags, needles, syringes, etc.* If not disposed of correctly, these will soon cause an even greater environmental disaster. When efforts to ensure enough vaccines, medicines, hospital beds, and even oxygen have been woefully inadequate, planning and executing the safe disposal of medical wastes have lost their place in the list of civic priorities.

Thirdly, while technological advancements made work from home and online education possible, the lockdown and the consequent restrictions have exposed the digital divide that cuts across the nation, creating

---

* PTI, 'India generated around 33,000 tonnes Covid-19 waste in 7 months: CPCB', *Business Standard*, 10 January 2021, https://www.business-standard.com/article/current-affairs/india-generated-around-33-000-tonnes-covid-19-waste-in-7-months-cpcb-121011000176_1.html.

new inequalities. Several critical services, such as banking, e-commerce, telemedicine, and e-governance, were accessible only via the Internet, leaving those without connectivity left out in the cold. Even though India had over 1,160 million wireless subscribers as of February 2020,* these numbers only account for essential internet services, with ownership of devices such as laptops, tablets, and smartphones being far lower in number. There is a gender divide in access, with 76 percent of men having access while the same is available to only 63 percent of women. Internet access and device ownership are not just a matter of economic choices but are also decided by socio-cultural beliefs and practices. An even greater danger that lurks is one of digital privacy. In the scramble to gain access to digital resources, we have perhaps ceded far too much of our personal information to tech conglomerates and even the government.[†]

Fourthly, economic hardships and social disintegration, polarizing caste, communal, and regional identities have resulted in a loss of individual well-being. The pandemic and the subsequent restrictions have dealt a heavy blow to personal

---

* Kundan Pandey, 'COVID-19 lockdown highlights India's great digital divide', *Down to Earth*, 30 July 2020, https://www.downtoearth. org.in/news/governance/covid-19-lockdown-highlights-india-s-great-digital-divide-72514#:~:text=Education%20is%20just%20 one%20area,via%20internet%20during%20the%20lockdown.

† Christophe Jaffrelot and Aditya Sharma, 'India's new digital rules are bad news for democracy', *Indian Express*, 4 March 2021.

freedom, safety from danger, and independence. The restrictions of lockdown and the consequent reduction in opportunities to earn a livelihood have curtailed individual agency in social and economic decision-making, both at a family and societal level. Unequal sharing of household chores, increased family care burden, and reduced financial capacity have made girls and women even more vulnerable. Social isolation has, in several cases, increased sexual and physical violence with little help from extended families or the community. Weaker sections, like the differently-abled and older people, find themselves even more dependent on others and less capable of managing their lives under these adverse circumstances.[*]

Finally, the rising number of Covid cases in 2021 compared to the previous year (1.75 times more daily cases than in September 2020) made survival a struggle. The costs of the pandemic on the economy have been a 10 percent fall in absolute GDP from the pre-pandemic trend level. We will also have to bear a permanent loss of 11 percent of GDP in real terms over the fiscal years 2021–22 through 2024–25.[†] Our World in Data, which mapped the percentage of the population in a country that lives on less than $30

---

[*] Aparna Joshi, 'COVID-19 pandemic in India: through psycho-social lens', Journal of Social and Economic Development 23 (2021): 414–37.

[†] Udit Misra, 'ExplainSpeaking: Will 2021 be a repear of 2020 for the Indian economy?', *Indian Express*, 31 May 2021.

a day (roughly an income of Rs 66,000 per month), has found the figure to be a whopping 99 percent in India. In comparison, it is only around 22 percent in the United States. Nevertheless, India has the world's third-highest number of billionaires, underlining our inequalities within.

The lockdown took away the daily earnings of millions in the informal sector. Due to a fall in demand, MSMEs had to shut down and operate at a lower capacity. This sector has been a significant employer but shows signs of a slow recovery, fearing that there may be future waves of the virus. India has around 308.3 million (112 million landless agricultural laborers, 45.7 million underprivileged self-employed in informal non-agricultural sectors, 150.6 million regular wage earners, and daily wagers in informal non-agricultural sectors). Their livelihoods are in severe peril and will continue to be so if the government does not incentivize the private sector to invest by offering tax breaks and increasing spending through MGNREGA (Mahatma Gandhi National Rural Employment Guarantee Act). Ironically, the government has allocated only Rs 73,000 crore for the financial year of 2021–22, which is lower than the actual expenditure of Rs 1.11 lakh crore in 2022–21.* This will, without a doubt, delay

---

* 'Budget: Centre allocates Rs 73,000 crore to MGNREGA - 34% less than revised estimate for 2020-'21', Scroll, 2 February 2021, https://scroll.in/latest/985693/budget-centre-allocates-rs-73000-crore-to-mgnrega-34-less-than-revised-estimate-for-2020-21.

wage payments and limit the scope of employment generation in the near future.

Time to awaken social consciousness?

During the weeks of the lockdown and months of working from home that followed, citizens blogged, tweeted, and Instagrammed how gradually the sky had cleared, the veil of fog had lifted, revealing the bright sun and even our 'sacred' rivers looked less murky having been spared from the influx of industrial effluents. The air had turned crisp, factories had paused their torrential pollution, and the traffic had ceased. Citizens spent hours trying to arrange transport for the migrants, packing meals and dry rations from their kitchens, and even raising their voices in indignation to wake up government officials. When everything has been bleak, many finally see that what makes a difference is a concern for the less fortunate and a realization that life should be lived in harmony with nature. The pandemic was, in a way, an opportunity to reconnect with an essential, innate quality—our social consciousness, our only hope in a dystopic world.

As a powerful and defining idea, social consciousness can be conceptualized as an individual's and an organization's moral obligation and commitment to preserve and improve societal welfare and its members' well-being. It involves having a sense of responsibility towards the underprivileged, the voiceless, and the marginalized and being accountable to all members of society. As corporates conduct their business in a socio-economic ecosystem, being sensitive to the expectations of a more extensive set of stakeholders, rather than just the shareholders, becomes imperative. Social consciousness is a moral force that aligns with organizational and societal interests and should be an underlying value that guides corporate mission, planning, and operations.

Socially conscious organizations: What do they look like?

The foremost quality-of-life issues that we face worldwide, and particularly in our country, of environmental pollution, increasing inequality, and economic stagnation can no longer be left to the government to solve but need cooperation and concerted efforts from the industry. Corporates that exist and thrive in the above milieu are part of a socio-economic-environmental intertwining that holds together differing stakeholders—customers, employees, laborers, vendors, and government. Being beneficiaries of the market, they implicitly shoulder the moral responsibility of designing and implementing corporate objectives in ways that align with various social, ethical, and environmentally conscious practices.

Social consciousness is a foundational and broad concept that needs to be differentiated from

Corporate Social Responsibility and Public Relations. CSR originally had a philanthropic beginning but is currently mandated by law. The amendment to Section 135 of the Companies Act 2013* requires qualifying Indian companies (net worth of Rs 5 billion or more/a turnover of Rs 10 billion or more/a net profit of Rs 50 million or more during the immediately preceding financial year) to spend in every financial year at least 2 percent of the company's average net profits made during the three immediately preceding financial years on CSR activities.† Such companies must establish a CSR committee and draft a CSR policy to guide their social investment. The amendment brought about a critical change, taking away the locus of social responsibility from the corporates and replacing it with a mandatory requirement. Social consciousness could be translated into social responsibility projects through the pathway of CSR but cannot be restricted to it. Social consciousness involves embedding stakeholder welfare in the organization's goals. While public relations are concerned with boundary-spanning activities of an organization and actions that enhance its brand

---

* Mohit Patel, 'Corporate Social Responsibility [From discretionary to disciplinary]', Tax Guru, 5 August 2019, https://taxguru.in/company-law/corporate-social-responsibility-from-discretionary-disciplinary.html.

† Neetika Ahuja, 'Analysing recent amendments to corporate social responsibility legislation', Lexology, 30 November 2020, https://www.lexology.com/library/detail.aspx?g=01e09bec-d194-4a11-a125-c2d3dc95be18.

image when assessed by the larger society, social consciousness is the wellspring of ideas, decisions, and actions concerning stakeholder welfare.

Social consciousness is a mindset that understands and accepts the interconnectedness of the economic, social, and natural worlds. In an increasingly intertwined and rapidly evolving world of organizations, boundaries of geographies have become porous. Economies and industries depend on natural forces and are severely affected by calamitous events. As organizations are embedded in, and are affected by, the external environment, sudden jolts and shocks in the environment have become sources of significant internal disruptions—the pandemic and its impact on businesses, industry, and employment bear testimony to this fact. Organizations have realized they can buffer themselves from environmental disruptions by building robust relationships with external stakeholders and strengthening interdependencies. Working together is the only feasible way forward.

World Economic Forum in April 2020 framed a set of 'Stakeholder Principles in the COVID Era' in consultation with several industry leaders. The key Stakeholder Principles are as follows:

To employees, our principle is to keep you safe: We will continue to do everything we can to protect your workplace and to help you to adapt to the new working conditions

To our ecosystem of suppliers and customers, our principle is to secure our shared business continuity: We will continue to work to keep supply chains open and integrate you into our business response.

To our end consumers, our principle is to maintain fair prices and commercial terms for essential supplies.

To governments and society, our principle is to offer our full support: We stand ready and will continue to complement public action with our resources, capabilities, and know-how.

To our shareholders, our principle remains the long-term viability of the company and its potential to create sustained value.

The World Economic Forum executive chairman Klaus Schwab has described the stakeholder principles as a real test for the stakeholder concept. He emphasized the need for such a proposal as an incapacity to deliver on the world's challenges as an interconnected society, such as climate change and social inclusion. Coming together is the only way to alleviate the pandemic's dire economic and social consequences.

https://www.weforum.org/press/2020/04/world-economic-forum-steps-up-coordinating-efforts-on-corporate-covid-responsewith various business leaders

Since social consciousness must be a corporate's guiding value and normative motive, its enactment rests with its leaders and managers. While corporates accept the need to be socially conscious, many need clarification on the behaviors and actions that constitute socially conscious management. The knowing–doing gap can be bridged only by making social consciousness a cultural mindset and aligning it with business strategy. The translation of social consciousness into organizational actions involves three steps:

Step One: Clarifying the normative values of concern for people (employees and external stakeholders), sustainability, and the environment. Articulating a mission statement and goals that ensure the embedding of social consciousness in the organization's psyche. Build a robust value-centered organizational culture.

Step Two: Disseminate the mission and goals, and dialogue with employees to align organizational goals with sustainability and environmental preservation. Conversations with employees are necessary to commit them to a meaningful purpose and be the flagbearers of socially responsible actions. In addition, the dialogue with employees creates an atmosphere of psychological safety wherein ideas can be challenged and co-created to achieve the mission. Further, the organization must set up internal systems to implement social responsibility, like a CSR committee of interested employees and a business innovation cell that encourages socially valuable innovations.

Step Three: Choose a pathway for achieving sustainability and environmental management goals. Through CSR, organizations can encourage employees to volunteer their time and efforts for social responsibility projects. Socially responsible business innovations are another pathway to convert social consciousness into societal accomplishments.

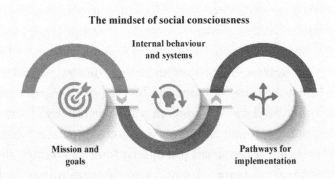

Figure 1: Processes for Embedding and Applying Social Consciousness

What would be the nature of conscious organizations, and what kind of practices identify one such? In their article on 'Conscious enterprise emergence: shared value creation through expanded conscious awareness', Kathryn Pavlovich and Patricia Doyle Corner explore how spiritual practices increase conscious awareness in entrepreneurs whose ventures build on shared values addressing social and community needs and profits for a larger social purpose. The article details several empirically validated practices that characterize socially conscious organizations.

Five core values form the mindset of a socially conscious organization: acting with care, being truthful, honest, using discretion, and not operating out of greed. Each of these values is translated into ways of interacting with employees and external stakeholders as below:

1. **Acting with care:** This includes treating various stakeholders like partners, suppliers, and customers with respect and compassion. The relational quality that underlies this relationship must be one of concern for the welfare of the other. Relational concern can be translated into organizational human resource practices like creating transparent job descriptions that concisely state the nature of work and responsibilities and transparent corporate systems, including fair and unbiased performance management systems. While setting goals for employees and targets for sales personnel, care must be taken in setting achievable goals rather than stretch goals whose achievement may necessitate adopting unethical means. The organizational culture should be risk-taking, allowing employees to experiment and innovate. Failures should be considered an opportunity to

learn and improve rather than punish, making employees risk-averse.

2. **Being truthful:** This is an essential requirement while communicating organizational expectations with partners, suppliers, distributors, and employees. It also emphasizes being truthful in communication with customers in advertisements. Another dimension of truthfulness is transparency in business practices involving employees and external stakeholders.

3. **Honesty:** Being an honest organization is described as the process of sharing the value created by a new venture with partners, suppliers, or customers. A socially conscious organization would also respect the intellectual capital of partners and suppliers. Further, by designing transparent human resource management systems, the organization would create an atmosphere of trust and one free from fear for employees.

4. **Use discretion:** Be restrained while negotiating with suppliers, potential business partners, and distributors by not driving a hard bargain that may be detrimental to the other party. Even though this may appear to be imprudent, it is a pragmatic choice that creates a win-win relationship that can last long. Employees are to be treated with compassion,

respect, and restraint. The organization must build collective support systems for employees rather than focus on individuals, fostering unhealthy competition.

5. **Absence of greed:** Socially conscious organizations must be generous towards their employees by paying them fair wages and hiring their services under fair employment practices. Generosity also needs to be extended toward suppliers, distributors, and customers. Finally, the absence of greed affirms not accepting bribes, gifts, or any other inducements.

In summary, social consciousness as a mindset creates pro-social intentions, which along with organizational processes like mission and goal setting, dialoguing with employees, and setting up internal systems, leads to choosing suitable pathways for action that lead to sustainable development. Sustainability expectations from corporates have changed over the years. Corporate sustainability 'embeds sustainability thinking deep into the corporate DNA and is viewed as a responsible and profitable way of management' (United Nations Global Compact [UNGC], 2014). Therefore, successful businesses must assess their actions' impact on the local and global community. Today, many corporates have rechristened their CSR function into corporate sustainability, allowing its influence to permeate all their functions—purchase, operations, finance, and marketing—and not be confined to the social responsibility department. Raw material sourcing, purchase, and production decisions are being considered in light of their 'green' impact and sustainability. This trend is gaining currency in no small measure due to changing consumer preferences favoring eco-friendly products.

Governance: The key to creating resilient and sustainable business strategies

BSR is an organization of sustainable business experts who provide insights and advice and help build collaborative sustainability initiatives for creating long-term business value and scale impact. Their mission is to work with businesses to create a just and sustainable world that can offer a prosperous and dignified life without plundering natural resources. The transformation of businesses needs a change in mindset and business transformation. BSR helps business leaders see the changes in the world more clearly and assists them in framing policy and implementing changes that can create long-term and sustainable value. In creating a culture of sustainability, the board plays a vital role in setting the sustainability agenda. To establish resilient business

strategies that can create long-term value, BSR
suggests the boards need to implement six key
innovations:

1. Emphasize long-term value creation over
   sustainability.
2. Strengthen   board   stewardship   of
   sustainability.
3. Align incentives to sustainability performance.
4. Recruit board members with expertise to
   guide the executive in understanding the
   strategic implications of sustainability issues.
5. Provide training on sustainability issues.
6. Create external advisory councils including
   relevant stakeholders.

https://www.bsr.org/en/our-insights/report-
view/redefining-sustainable-business-
management-for-a-rapidly-changing-

Impact Champions: What can they do?

Socially conscious organizations do not come into
existence without socially conscious managers. We
rechristen such managers Impact Champions as they have
the intent and capabilities to transform an organization
into a socially conscious one. Many harbor pro-social
inclinations during their student days; however, they

abandon them once they start a corporate career. In the 'big, bad world of corporates', where beating the competition and exceeding performance expectations are understood to be the basis for career advancement, they feel that their social ideals have no place. Some think of social consciousness as the responsibility of the top management and not theirs. Although deep in their heart, they feel the need for socially conscious action from corporates they work with, most give a helpless shrug and say, 'What can we do?'

We say, 'a lot'. Yes, it definitely helps to have a top managerial position to push an organizational transformation agenda forward. Nevertheless, more than just the top management has driven social plans in the corporate world. Besides, the corporate sector is expected to respond more to societal and environmental causes. Several corporates already have generous budgets and tailored programs to support such causes. Therefore, young managers will have a good chance of successfully pursuing socially conscious action in the corporate sector.

An Impact Champion is an intrapreneur committed to using business as a powerful force for doing good inside existing organizations. She may take on the role of an entrepreneur creating a social enterprise for solving social problems if constrained by organizational boundaries.

We need young managers who step into the roles of Impact Champions. Acting internally in the organization, they work as social intrapreneurs who sincerely believe in the idea of sharing value and have the confidence that they can enact their social consciousness to make a positive impact on the world using their ideas, skills, actions, and organizational resources they have access to. As more and more managers participate in the dialogue and initiate pro-social action, social consciousness will be institutionalized as part of the organizational culture.

One of the critical behaviors of an Impact Champion is self-labeling, reinforcing one's commitment to the larger purpose. Self-labeling comprises a genuine belief in one's agency to be a changemaker and an internal moral compass that guides action toward societal good over corporate profit. Self-labeling further generates clarity and confidence for dialoguing with and convincing others of the need for a broader perspective on growth and success that incorporates sustainable development goals into business planning. As an initiator of new ideas, an impact champion has to be internally driven. Such passion and sincerity would be capable of galvanizing action at three levels—employees (micro), organizational (meso), and societal (macro) levels for the effectuation of inclusive and sustainable growth.

The role description (we use the word *role* as the terminology as it is a function *assumed by the individual* rather than one that the organization *assigns*) of an Impact Champion would include the three key roles:

Idea champion: Organizations do not innovate; instead, individuals do. As a generator of ideas, an Impact Champion inspires, encourages, and helps jumpstart others with ideas on incorporating sustainability and social good in business strategy and implementation. An Impact Champion is a creative and collaborative individual who helps others develop a social innovation mindset.

Change agent: Three attributes that a successful Impact Champion must possess are: firstly, the self-concept of being a change agent and self-efficacy for the role; secondly, the knowledge about economic, social, and environmental issues that plague society and could affect business viability and survival in the long term; and thirdly the skills for bringing about the change such as networking and building trust among stakeholders, persuasiveness, and ability to manage ambiguity and uncertainty.

Coalition builder: To address complex problems of depletion of natural resources, calamitous events like the current pandemic, and economic and social disruptions, to name a few, we need the cooperative efforts of several stakeholders whose goals and concerns are interconnected. An Impact Champion is the central communicator, collaboration enabler, and coordinator who gathers disparate groups under an umbrella to deliberate on their common problems and evolve solutions that benefit each.

Pathways for an Impact Champion

An Impact Champion faces the challenging task of introducing, embedding, and maintaining a social mindset that serves the long-term interest of society, being consistent with the organization's core business objectives. Such a fundamental change in attitude needs to be supported by an organizational transformation of business processes, redefining customer segments to be served, and training employees in sustainability and social responsibility practices. This raises the question: how do we do this?

We suggest three pathways for an Impact Champion in this book: (1) Corporate Social Responsibility, (2) Corporate Social Innovation, and (3) Social Entrepreneurship. These pathways are alternative routes for undertaking socially conscious action and making a social impact. Each individual can choose any path depending on their inclinations and circumstances. The first two pathways can be pursued within the organization, and the third is more likely outside the organization, however, within the business ecosystem itself. The level of challenge in execution and the extent of personal investment of time, skills, and resources progressively increase from Pathways 1 to 3.

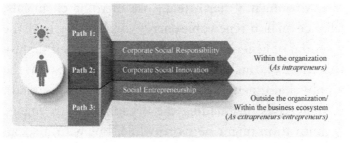

Pathway 1: Corporate Social Responsibility (CSR)

Most corporates support CSR activities. CSR probably is the most accessible pathway to get started on for socially conscious individuals to make a social impact. Where there are pre-existing CSR departments and programs, they can volunteer with them and participate in their activities. In organizations with rudimentary CSR or where the current CSR activities do not address pressing social issues close to the individual's heart, they can initiate newer actions under the CSR umbrella. Since CSR is widely recognized as a legitimate corporate activity by internal and external stakeholders, getting them off the ground is relatively easy. As corporates often view CSR as good PR opportunities, securing organizational support may be easy.

Pathway 2: Corporate Social Innovation (CSI)

CSR does not typically involve changing the corporate's business practices and models. One might observe that it is these business models that are creating social or environmental harm (e.g., use of toxic chemicals, reliance on non-renewable energy) or that they have the potential of generating more societal benefits if slightly altered (e.g., including marginalized groups in the supply chain, new products for the old and disabled). In such cases, persuading the organization to engage in innovation might be worthwhile, but with a social focus rather than serving corporate interests alone. Although such Corporate Social Innovations may have created positive outcomes for the organization, they are likely to require hard-sell compared to CSR projects. They will require buy-in from various internal and external stakeholders, who must be prepared to share and invest in resources and change their internal processes, technology, and business models.

Pathway 3: Social Entrepreneurship (SE)

The evolution of the social entrepreneurship space in India is replete with examples of socially conscious intrapreneurs who, after a few years of building a sustainability ethos in their organizations, left employment to start their social enterprise where they had much greater leeway to execute their ideas and conviction. Those who pursue this path are usually interested in solving social and environmental problems that fall outside the scope of the CSR or CSI initiatives of the organization(s) they worked with. They might also be driven by the desire to create their entrepreneurial venture. They could launch this as social entrepreneurs if they could galvanize corporate support. They leverage their experience, skills, and networks to kickstart the social enterprise.

In this book, we cover all three pathways in three parts. While each involves complexities and processes, which will require an entire book to explain, we intend this book to be a primer to familiarize the reader with each and give deeper insight into specific essential aspects. The aim is to help the reader choose a pathway that suits them best to enact their social consciousness and make a social impact.

2

Society and Development: Corporate Partnerships for Equitable and Sustainable Growth

Saving the precious drops—together

Water, the source and sustenance of life, is getting depleted too fast! NITI Aayog, in its 2018 report, has warned us that nearly half our population will face extreme water scarcity in the next decade. We are one of the world's biggest groundwater extractors, and most of our freshwater sources and major river have been contaminated by industrial effluents and sewage.

Most developmental aspirations depend on a steady water supply, without which our cities will become uninhabitable, shutting industries and livelihoods and displacing people. A quarter of India's population still practices open defecation, contributing to water-borne illness and even death.

The Swatch Bharat Abhiyan launched in 2014 to make India ODF is still a work in progress as the millions of toilets built can be used only if they have access to water. Water scarcity has burdened women unequally; they having to spend hours collecting water for the household.

Research informs us that most water depletion is not caused by industrial or household consumption but rather by water-intensive agriculture that has guzzled groundwater without replenishment. Inadequate rainfall and increasing spells of dry monsoon days should be warning enough for us to consider seriously conserving every drop of rainwater and recycling wastewater.

A ray of hope lies in collaboration—between government and farmers, piecing together innovative, cost-effective water conservation solutions. One such example is farmers' digging of 10,000 farm ponds across villages under the guidance of a district collector in Madhya Pradesh. The ponds helped store monsoon water, increase crop yield, and diversify crops grown, enhancing farm productivity and earnings. Hindustan Zinc Limited (HZL) established a PPP with the Udaipur Municipal Corporation (UMC) and the Rajasthan Urban Improvement Trust in 2012 and built Udaipur's first sewage treatment plant that aimed at treating 100 percent of Udaipur's domestic sewage by 2022. CETP (Thane–Belapur) Association, a non-profit-making Section 8 company established in 1994, is a single-point treatment facility for industrial waste from medium and small-scale enterprises in the Thane–Belapur belt. Adjudged as 'one of the best-run CETP in India,' the plant has been serving 572 small-scale and 91 medium/large-scale members of the Thane–Belapur Industrial Association (TBIA) and has 2,582 non-members as users. This successful model is being replicated across Maharashtra.

Conserving and managing a scarce resource like water requires all hands to come together, government, non-profits, corporates, and civic society. They have to act together and fast!

Sources:

https://water.org/our-impact/where-we-work/india/

https://www.indiatoday.in/magazine/cover-story/story/20210329-the-great-indian-thirst-1781280-2021-03-20

https://www.firstpost.com/tech/science/indias-water-crisis-bengaluru-delhi-chennai-hyderabad-among-21-cities-to-run-out-of-groundwater-by-2020-4590221.html

https://www.orfonline.org/research/arresting-indias-water-crisis-the-economic-case-for-wastewater-use/

https://cetpttc.org/

~

The 2019 Global Wealth Databook* from Credit Suisse reports that 73 percent of Indians have a net worth of less than $10,000 (compared to just 19 percent in China), while 2.3 percent have a net worth of over $1 million. India ranks fourth in the world after the USA, China, and Germany in ultra-high-net-worth individuals (4,593), making us one of the fastest-growing and most unequal nations.

Economic and social inequity is not an India-specific phenomenon. The World Social Report 2020[†] by the United Nations underlines the need to tackle poverty and deeply entrenched inequalities in basic needs like safe water, sanitation and healthcare, clean energy, and income-generating opportunities. Climate change disproportionately impacts the poor, exposing their livelihoods to the vagaries of weather. Inequity breeds frustration, and the ensuing discontentment can destabilize communities and governments, decelerating development and growth. Therefore, building an equitable and just society is often considered an economic and moral imperative for the world.

Addressing developmental inequities and strengthening our social and environmental

---

* 'Global Wealth Databook 2019', Credit Suisse Research Institute, October 2019, https://www.credit-suisse.com/about-us/en/reports-research/global-wealth-report.html.
† 'World Social Report 2020', Department of Economic and Social Affairs, United Nations, https://www.un.org/development/desa/dspd/wp-content/uploads/sites/22/2020/01/World-Social-Report-2020-FullReport.pdf.

infrastructure is the only practical option. Access to food, water, healthcare, and education are commonly understood as 'poor' people's problems. They are the first to be hit, that too very hard—no doubt. It was seen in the first pandemic wave that swept through India. The middle class and above do not see themselves as beneficiaries of the public infrastructure and believe they can afford to access necessities such as food, water, healthcare, and education by private means and from the private sector. The second wave of the pandemic showed us how false that sense of security is! With the relatively well-off scrambling for medical care, medicines, oxygen, and ventilators, it became apparent that none of us will be spared from the ill effects of our developmental shortcomings. One may be tempted to disregard the pandemic as a black swan event, the probability of which is very low.

Nevertheless, we cannot disregard the warnings of the irreversible changes, such as decreasing water tables that will make drinking water inaccessible in our cities like Bangalore,* which will affect both the poor and the rich. This is no longer *poor people's problem*. It is *everybody's problem*.

This also shows that it is everybody's responsibility to address them. Developmental challenges are usually left for the government and NGOs to tackle. If we

---

* S. Vishwanath, 'Bengaluru's water story: Can the paradise be regained?', *The Hindu*, 21 June 2020, https://www.thehindu.com/news/cities/bangalore/our-water-story-can-the-paradise-be-regained/article31881200.ece.

were to take cues from the pandemic, it is evident that neither the public nor private sector can do it alone. The pandemic has brought to the surface the interconnectedness and mutual dependencies of the multiple sectors and actors. It would take all of them working together if we were to ensure our survival.

This chapter outlines the global and national level efforts to address various developmental challenges that humanity must collectively address. We provide a status update on where India stands at the policy level. These are areas where the corporate sector actors can meaningfully contribute. It is for aspiring Impact Champions to draw the attention of their organizations to these areas, devise initiatives and forge partnerships to address them.

The global call for action

Globally, the call to action has been made to tackle global development challenges and climate change while ensuring a better deal for the marginalized and impoverished. Interestingly, these efforts began to emerge under various UN bodies at around the same time the nations world over were being integrated under WTO treaties into a global economy, to be primarily governed by free-market principles. The notable initiatives included the first-ever UN Conference on Environment and Development (commonly known as Rio Earth Summit) in 1992 and the World Summit on Social Development in Copenhagen in 1995.

The various ideas around social development from such forums led to the development of Millennium Development Goals towards the end of the decade.

Under the aegis of the United Nations (UNDP mainly through its association with 170 member countries), the Millennium Development Goals had since 2000 attempted to forge a global partnership to reduce inequality and ensure a life of dignity for the poor and dispossessed. A progress review in 2015, the deadline for MDG, took stock of the impact of global action and recommended that concerted efforts need to continue in the form of seventeen sustainable development goals to be fulfilled in fifteen years. The SDGs' key feature is the understanding and agreement that the plans will be achievable by 2030 only through the concerted, collaborative efforts of the private sector, civic society, and governments.

The Indian response

India is a signatory to SDGs and has committed to achieving specific goals by 2030. NITI Ayog acts as the public body that coordinates government schemes and other multi-sectoral partnerships to achieve these goals and track progress. While the government has taken the lead with various programs and schemes, the corporates have pitched in by mapping their corporate social responsibility (CSR) efforts to SDGs, ensuring they spend wisely and help the nation progress towards the globally committed milestones. We also see corporates

going beyond CSR and introducing the business model
and technological innovation to achieve SDG targets.
In addition, there has been a rapid increase in social
enterprises in India developing innovative ways of
tackling persistent wicked problems.

The ground reality

A more in-depth analysis of our introductory example
(in Chapter 1) of the migrant labor exodus reveals several
socio-economic factors interlinked in causing such an
arduous journey. Industrial development in India has
been lopsided, forcing people from underdeveloped
states with fewer job opportunities to relocate to other
states for livelihood. The 2011 census had put the total
number of migrant laborers at a staggering 37 percent
of the country's population.* By 2019, 29 percent of
the people in cities were migrant daily wage earners
(CSDS, APU).† Freakish, unpredictable weather
conditions, increasing water scarcity, crop failures,
and unremunerative prices due to exploitative market
conditions make agriculture financially unviable and
deter farmers from encouraging their wards to take
up farming. This is ironic because if agriculture has to
progress from subsistence to intensive, has to enhance

---

* Sushant Singh and Aanchal Magazine, 'Explained: Indian migrants,
  across India', *Indian Express*, 6 April 2020, https://indianexpress.
  com/article/explained/coronavirus-india-lockdown-migran-
  workers-mass-exodus-6348834/.
† Ibid.

productivity using agro-tech interventions and diversify the variety of crops grown, it will need qualified and involved youth, not apathetic ones. The world over, agriculture has prospered in no small measure due to advances in food processing capabilities and a robust cold chain for transportation. However, Indian farmers still lack sufficient post-harvest storage for their products and cold chains to access retail markets. Inadequate food processing facilities have offered them little incentive to switch to high-value crops.

India has witnessed a tremendous expansion in its working-age (20–50 years) population, estimated at approximately 63 percent. The fruits of this demographic dividend will be evident only if the manufacturing sector absorbs this cohort. Such an uptake requires labor to be educated/ vocationally skilled for manufacturing, which, unfortunately, is not the case. The government set up the National Skills Development Council in 2008 for skilling/upskilling 500 million people by 2022* in partnership with private training institutes. Though it continues to catalyze skill development, fundamental challenges like poor nutrition and inadequate healthcare have kept the rural workforce suboptimal. We face the enormous task of tackling urban and rural development without

---

* 'Role of Manufacturing in Employment Generation in India', India Brand Equity Foundation, https://www.ibef.org/download/Role-of-Manufacturing-in-Employment-Generation-in-India.pdf.

depleting resources and polluting the environment. The enormity, urgency, and criticality of the challenge make it ripe for corporations, social sectors, and government to collaborate to achieve growth with equity.

What is India doing?

> 'The focus (on restarting the economy) is on select industries, farming, and rural employment guarantee program.'
>
> —Punya Salila Srivastava,
> Joint Secretary, Home Ministry.

Since the unlocking of the economy after the first wave of the pandemic, the central government announced a revitalization plan with Rs 20 lakh crore allocated to promote rural livelihood*for making the country Atmanirbhar. The Indian government aims to encourage a transition to a manufacturing-led economy rather than a service-led one as the route to large-scale employment generation. The idea is to cut the bureaucratic red tape by creating an empowered group of secretaries in various ministries and Project

---

* Aditya Kumar, 'Summary of announcements: Aatma Nirbhar Bharat Abhiyaan', PRS Legislative Research, 20 May 2020, https://www.prsindia.org/report-summaries/summary-announcements-aatma-nirbhar-bharat-abhiyaan.

Development Cells (PDCs) for speedy clearance of investment proposals.[*]

However, achieving sustainable rural development will involve disentangling social, economic, and environmental challenges that plague rural areas. Poverty, consequent malnutrition, poor health, and lack of education have kept the quality of rural human resources abysmally low. Therefore, any productivity improvement will require a multi-pronged intervention—in education and vocational training, health care, employment guarantees, and vastly improved infrastructure. Government policies are on offers, such as the Swachh Bharat Mission and Pradhan Mantri Awas Yojana (for WASH and housing), Beti Bacho Beti Padhao (for gender equity), Pradhan Mantri Jan Dhan Yojana (for economic upliftment), and Deen Dayal Upadhyay Gram Jyoti Yojana and Pradhan Mantri Ujjwala Yojana (for energy and electrification) that are meant to integrate economic, gender, and environmental aspects of development.

State governments, particularly those whose citizens comprise a majority of migrant labor, have announced industrialization schemes by enticing industry with production-based incentives and offering emergency credit guarantees. Madhya Pradesh, Assam, Odisha,

---

[*] 'India forms empowered group to attract investments, milk opportunities in post-Covid world', *Hindustan Times*, 3 June 2020, https://www.hindustantimes.com/india-news/india-forms-empowered-group-to-attract-investments-milk-opportunities-in-post-covid-world/story-hTO7SUEYYocWnsipx2VX3K.html.

Punjab, Haryana, and Andhra Pradesh are all vying for investments by offering subsidized electricity, quick clearances, and other sops. For instance, Uttar Pradesh has set up land banks comprising excess government lands in fourteen districts leased to industry.* Industrial parks are being commissioned to attract foreign investments, small and medium enterprises (MSMEs), particularly micro food enterprises (MFEs), and dairy plants are being set up. Beekeeping, floriculture, and herb cultivation are being incentivized. They offer to resolve investor complaints on a war footing to improve the ease of doing business as part of a multi-pronged revival strategy.† Industry representative body CII, in its June 2020 conference on building India, reiterated the need to focus on lives, livelihood, and growth.‡ The reverse migration necessitated geographically distributed development models against a city-centric model and more significant investment in digital technology, infrastructure, and healthcare. This is the most opportune moment for corporates to realize the value of a multi-faced developmental initiative such as the SDGs and thus contribute to resilient and inclusive growth.

---

* 'UP preparing land banks for industries in 14 districts', *Daily Pioneer*, https://www.dailypioneer.com/2020/state-editions/up-preparing-land-banks--for-industries-in-14-dists.html.

† Ibid.

‡ 'CII bats for multi-pronged strategy to revive economy', *Tribune*, 20 June 2020, https://www.tribuneindia.com/news/amritsar/cii-bats-for-multi-pronged-strategy-to-revive-economy-101786.

Working toward Sustainable Development Goals

The Sustainable Development Goals have been crafted around three core foci-economic progress, taking everyone along the developmental path, ensuring that economic progress is achieved sustainably, and conserving resources for future generations while building a stable and prosperous society. For example, a growing child in a rural village needs nutrition and timely immunization to achieve initial developmental milestones. This necessitates a steady income for the parents, clean drinking water, and healthcare, not to mention good maternal health, which is essential for a decent head start in the child's life. A school with quality teachers and midday meals will ensure that the child learns well and is prepared to advance into higher education. Nevertheless, the reality of rural India is rather bleak. For instance, the shortage of qualified medical professionals is so acute that it stalled the Ayushman Bharat Yojana implementation in 2018.* Informal providers, i.e., professionals with no formal medical training, comprise 68 percent of rural healthcare in rural India.† A 2019 NSO Survey revealed that 25 percent of rural households did not have access to sanitation facilities, imperiling the quality of water they draw from wells.‡ In 2017, less than 50 percent of Indians had access to safely managed drinking water (UNICEF, 2019).§ Even more alarming is that around two-thirds of our 718 districts face acute groundwater depletion due to the indiscriminate use of bore wells, exposing us to acute shortages in the immediate future. In 2019, the Ministry of Drinking Water and Sanitation was renamed as Jal Shakti Ministry, with a view to decentralize water management with the help of communities involved in planning and implementing Swajal Water Supply Schemes.

---

* Devyani Chhetri, 'India's Villages Don't Have Enough Health Workers. But Here Is How Modicare's Wellness Drive Can Still Succeed', India Spend, 18 October 2018, https://www.indiaspend.com/indias-villages-dont-have-enough-health-workers-but-here-is-how-modicares-wellness-drive-can-still-succeed/.

† Jishnu Das et al., 'Two Indias: The structure of primary health care markets in rural Indian villages with implications for policy', *Social Science & Medicine*, 301 (2022): 112799.

‡ Neetu Chandra Sharma, '25% of rural India's households don't have access to sanitation: NSO survey', *Mint*, 25 November 2019, https://www.livemint.com/news/india/25-of-rural-india-s-households-don-t-have-access-to-sanitation-nso-survey-11574690136848.html.

§ 'Clean Drinking Water', UNICEF, https://www.unicef.org/india/what-we-do/clean-drinking-water.

The pandemic has dealt a deadly blow to an already fragile education system, reports the Annual State of Education Report (ASER) survey* (Sept 2020), leaving 20 percent of rural children without textbooks, around 70 percent with no learning materials or activities provided by their schools, and only 10 percent with access to live online classes. Parental incapability in tutoring their wards and lack of digital technology access has widened the inequity chasm.

India's developmental agenda is supposed to be driven by the idea of 'Sabka Saath, Sabka Vikas,' meaning Collective Effort, Inclusive Development. Therefore, understanding the interlinkages between the various SDGs will help direct government and corporate efforts toward a regionally balanced, inclusive, and sustainable development.

In the section below, we enumerate some noteworthy schemes introduced for bridging the resource gap in livelihood, healthcare, and education and the programs that aim to foster economic development that is respectful of the environment, energy-efficient, and sustainable.

---

* 'Nearly 20% of rural school children had no textbooks due to COVID-19 impact, finds ASER survey', *The Hindu*, 28 October 2020, https://www.thehindu.com/news/national/coronavirus-20-of-rural-school-children-had-no-textbooks-due-to-covid-19-impact-finds-aser-survey/article32966299.ece.

Ensuring the Essentials: No Povery, Zero Hunger, Good Health and Well-Being, Clean Water and Sanitation

Ensuring essentials involves providing necessities like food, water, sanitation, and healthcare and making them available to the poor. Globally, poverty is recognized as a multidimensional phenomenon and an acceptance of the many kinds of depravities that define it has gone a

SDGs

1, 2, 3 & 6

long way in helping governments identify the deserving and chalk out poverty alleviation measures. Lacking access to safe drinking water, inadequate sanitation, ill health, lack of education, geographical isolation, political exclusion, and inequity due to social status, caste, gender, and sexual orientation are all disadvantages that make people vulnerable to poverty. Multiple poverty alleviation programs address each one of them.

India has significantly reduced deprivations in nutrition, child mortality, drinking water, and sanitation (Gaur and Rao, 2020). Several social welfare programs have helped achieve this outcome. Prominent among them are the Mahatma Gandhi National Rural Employment Guarantee Act* (MGNREGA) which guarantees a minimum of 100 days of wage employment per household every year for the rural

---

* The Mahatma Gandhi National Rural Employment Guarantee Act 2005, https://nrega.nic.in/MGNREGA_new/Nrega_home.aspx.

unskilled workers, and the National Rural Livelihoods Mission* that promotes self-employment among the rural poor. The Pradhan Mantri Jan-Dhan Yojana (PMJDY) supplements these programs[†] that provides the rural poor with financial services like banking, credit, insurance, and pension. On the healthcare front, the Pradhan Mantri Jan Arogya Yojana-Ayushman Bharat[‡] offers free healthcare to 10 crore households just as better health through cleanliness and ending open defecation are the objectives of the Swachh Bharat Mission[§] (Clean India Mission). The National Rural Drinking Water Programme augments good health by ensuring that around 75 percent of our population gets 40 liters of drinking water supply per capita per day. Macro-level initiatives like the National River Conservation Programme[¶] (NRCP), the Namami Gange–Integrated Conservation Mission, and the scheme to interlink rivers are envisaged to safeguard this precious resource.

Hunger has been hunted down by the Public Distribution System that supplies 800 million people

---

* Deendayal Antyodaya Yojana–National Rural Livelihoods Mission, https://www.aajeevika.gov.in/.
† Pradhan Mantri Jan Dhan Yojana (PMJDY), https://pmjdy.gov.in/.
‡ Pradhan Mantri Jan Arogya Yojana (PM-JAY), https://pmjay.gov.in/.
§ Swachh Bharat Mission, https://swachhbharatmission.gov.in/sbmcms/index.htm.
¶ National River Conservation Directorate, https://nrcd.nic.in/.

with food grains at affordable prices.* The Mid-Day
Meal Programme provides nutritious cooked meals to
over 11.59 crore children in primary schools aiding
their cognitive development and physical growth. The
National Health Policy (2017) complements these
efforts, striving to universalize primary health care,
reduce infant mortality and prevent death due to
non-communicable diseases. Giving special attention
to children is the Integrated Child Development
Scheme (ICDS). The scheme is akin to an umbrella
encompassing maternal and infant health, nutrition,
and preschool education. Of the several related
programs, the Janani Suraksha Yojana[†] (JSY)
encourages institutional deliveries and better maternal
care through cash transfers. At the same time, Mission
Indradhanush covers immunizing children who have
not been vaccinated. The Bal Swasthya Karyakram
undertakes early diagnosis of disorders and disabilities
and offers free-of-cost intervention for children up
to age eighteen. Together, these centrally sponsored
programs have been designed to bolster the health of
our future generation.

---

* N. A. George and F. H. McKay, 'The Public Distribution System
  and Food Security in India', *International Journal of Environmental
  Research and Public Health*, 16(17), (2019): 3221.
† 'Janani Suraksha Yojana', National Health Mission, https://nhm.
  gov.in/index1.php?lang=1&level=3&sublinkid=841&lid=309.

Education, Equality, and Empowerment: Quality Education, Gender Equality, and Reduced Inequalities

A nation advances based on the quality of its human resources. The Right to Education Act* is a significant step toward improving the quality of our human resources  through free and compulsory education for children (aged between 6 to 14 years), confirming equity and non-discrimination by opening the doors of private schools to underprivileged children from the neighborhood. The National Education Mission[†] combines four programs (viz. Saakshar Bharat, Sarva Shiksha Abhiyan, Rashtriya Madhyamik Shiksha Abhiyan, and Scheme on Teacher Education), a multi-pronged effort to improve access to education for all, lower learning-related and gender-based inequities. Additionally, governmental support is also in place for teachers' training and education for adults, girls, people with disabilities, minorities, and ST students.

A social issue that continues to be a cause for concern is gender-based violence, beginning with prenatal sex determination testing, followed by female feticide and infanticide widely reported in several

---

* 'About', Right to Education, https://righttoeducation.in/know-your-rte/about.
† 'National Education Mission', Wikipedia, https://en.wikipedia.org/wiki/National_Education_Mission.

states.* The Indian government passed the Pre-Conception and Prenatal Diagnostic Techniques Act (PCPNDT) in 1994, banning prenatal sex screening and making it a punishable offense. The Equal Remuneration Act of 1973 and the Maternity Benefit Act of 1961 aid working women by acknowledging their right to equal wages and benefits during early motherhood. Indira Gandhi Matritva Sahyog Yojana, Rajiv Gandhi Scheme for Empowerment of Adolescent Girls (SABLA), Beti Bachao Beti Padhao, and Sukanya Samridhi Yojana (Girl Child Prosperity Scheme) form part of the arsenal to protect girls and ensure that opportunities for education and advancement are made accessible to them. While support for Training and Employment Programme for Women (STEP) helps improve employability, the Sexual Harassment of Women at Workplace (Prevention, Prohibition and Redressal) Act, 2013 aims to ensure safe workplaces for women.

Empowerment of the dispossessed, socially and economically marginalized is essential to help them escape the depths of despair they have been relegated to for decades. The government has sought to achieve this through multi-sectoral development programs for minorities, offering grants to backward regions, assistance schemes for scheduled caste development

* Sravani Sarkar, 'About 4.6 crore females 'missing' in India due to son preference: UNFPA report', *The Week*, 1 July 2020, https://www.theweek.in/news/india/2020/07/01/about-46-crore-females-missing-in-india-due-to-son-preference-unfpa-report.html.

corporations, and loans to support micro-enterprises (e.g., the Pradhan Mantri MUDRA Yojana).*

Enhanced Economic Development: Affordable Clean Energy, Decent Work and Economic Growth, Industry, Innovation, and Infrastructure, Responsible Consumption and Production

The crux of a nation's advancement lies in its people's economic prosperity. Industrialization and manufacturing are sought to be boosted through support for setting

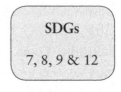

SDGs

7, 8, 9 & 12

up enterprises. The Make in India drive was launched to make India a hub for global manufacturing; Start-Up India aims to ease setting up companies through handholding, funding support, incentives, and industry-academia partnership for technology and idea exchanges. The government's Ease of Doing Business initiative has introduced e-payment and e-business portals, e-courts for enforcing contracts, e-procurement modules to sell to the government, and GST, reducing the multiplicity of indirect taxes procedures of payment uniform and straightforward. Interventions like the National Handloom Development Programme, Catalytic Development Programme for Sericulture,

---

* Pradhan Mantri MUDRA Yojana (PMDY), https://www.mudra.org.in/.

and the Border Area Development Programme target specific sectors and regions.

The National Skill Development Mission aids sustained economic advancement, and the interests of workers in the unorganized sector are taken care of by the social security schemes like the Rashtriya Swastya Bima Yojana and the Deendayal Upadhyaya Antodaya Yojana.

Industrial development can only be sustained with clean fuels. The government has set up renewable energy projects as public-private-partnership, adding additional capacity to fuel the nation's growth needs. The National Solar Mission and the National Mission for Enhanced Energy Efficiency help reduce our dependence on fossil fuels. A national policy on biofuels has suggested a 20 percent blending of biofuels with fossil-based ones by 2030, reducing reliance on imports and boosting electricity production from non-fossil fuels to 40 percent.* Finally, the quest to reduce energy's carbon intensity drives the National Clean Energy Fund[†] to fund clean energy research.

---

* 'National Policy on Biofuels 2018: Here are key things you should know', *Economic Times*, 5 November 2019, https://economictimes. indiatimes.com/small-biz/productline/power-generation/national-policy-on-biofuels-2018-here-are-key-things-you-should-know/articleshow/71922729.cms?from=mdr.

[†] National Clean Energy Fund, https://doe.gov.in/sites/default/files/NCEF%20Brief_post_BE_2017-18.pdf.

*Sustainable Life: Climate Change, Life below
Water, Life on Land, Sustainable Communities*

Assessing climate change over the
Indian region, the Union Ministry
of Earth Sciences has set off
warning bells of rising temperature
that seriously impacts biodiversity.

SDGs

13, 14 & 15

Rising temperatures and reduced rainfall can wreak havoc
with agriculture, our mainstay, affect the Himalayas,
and imperil our energy security. The National Action
Plan on Climate Change and its eight missions aim to
stymie climate change by influencing key initiatives that
industry and non-government actors are engaged in.

The National Plan for Conservation of Aquatic
Ecosystems (NPCA) leads a holistic conservation
program for lakes and wetlands to improve water
quality and expand biodiversity. Conservation of
aquatic resources needs to be complemented by building
sewerage treatment plants and other infrastructure in
towns and cities so that sewage sludge does not seep
into the ground or drain into rivers. Despite the zeal
to improve cleanliness and sanitation, there needs to
be more innovation in the government's management
of septage sludge. The Atal Mission for Rejuvenation
and Urban Transformation* (AMRUT) forms the

---

* 'Atal Mission for Rejuvenation and Urban Transformation -
  AMRUT', Ministry of Housing and Urban Affairs, https://mohua.
  gov.in/cms/amrut.php.

institutional foundation of critical sewerage and septage management, charged with setting up sewage treatment plants and ensuring they function.

An antidote to climate change is afforestation. The National Afforestation Programme develops forest resources with people's participation while helping the poor in the forest-fringe communities to continue to live in harmony with the forests. In addition, the Integrated Development of Wild Life Habitats offers assistance in setting up and managing wildlife sanctuaries and habitats. Another vital policy is the National Action Programme to Combat Desertification, which integrates watershed management to conserve and redevelop degraded natural resources and afforestation to replenish green cover.

Increasing urbanization necessitates efficient utilization of energy and waste management. The Jawaharlal Nehru National Urban Renewal Mission,* a city modernization scheme, aims to create equitable, efficient cities with affordable education and health care for the urban poor governed by the municipalities. Also under its purview is the renewal of old cities to reduce congestion in new ones. To safeguard rural areas from being left behind, the Pradhan Mantri Adarsh Gram

---

* 'Jawaharlal Nehru National Urban Renewal Mission', Ministry of Housing and Urban Affairs, https://mohua.gov.in/cms/jawaharlal-nehru-national-urban-renewal-mission.php.

Yojana (PMAGY),* an area-based developmental program, focuses on the integrated development of villages where more than half the people belong to the scheduled castes. These facilities and opportunities are intended to narrow the gap between the SCs and others.

Peace and Partnership: Peace, Justice, and Strong Institutions, Partnership for the Goals

The cornerstone of a growing nation is an environment that ensures institutional arrangements like the army, judiciary, and police assure people's and property's

SDGs

16 & 17

safety and security. The freedom to follow a trade or vocation of one's choice necessitates a society liberated from discrimination and suppression. Though India's constitution protects and guarantees us our fundamental rights (e.g., the right to equality, freedom, education, and protection against exploitation), several other rights are enforced by law. Unfortunately, the country's legal system does not inspire much confidence in the common citizen as justice had been severely delayed, if not entirely unserved. A 2018 government report has estimated the backlog in Indian courts as being 60,000 cases pending in Supreme Court, 42 lakh

---

* Pradhan Mantri Adarsh Gram Yojana (PMAGY), http://www. pmagy.gov.in/aboutPMAGY.

cases in different high courts, and around 2.7 crore cases in district and subordinate courts.*

Further, the ease of doing business is adversely affected by the pendency of cases relating to contract enforcement. To hasten the disposal of cases, the government set up 1,734 Fast Track Courts in 2000, an inadequate number, as ideally, for the 718 districts in India, the number of FTCs required would be around 3,000. A review after years revealed that only 1,562 were functioning. A recent report suggests that about fifteen states and union territories do not have even a single functioning FTC.† Governmental provisions continue to ease the gridlock, including setting up the PRAGATI (Pro-Active Governance and Timely Implementation) Platform in 2015. This multi-modal, multipurpose digital platform brings together the PMO, Union government secretaries, and the state's chief secretaries to redress the common person's grievances.

Another threat to development is the corruption and bribery in public services, and government departments meant to facilitate industry and business. In their July 2020 report,‡ Transparency International

---

* 'Judicial backlog: How India can end the long wait for justice', DailyO, 5 May 2018, ttps://www.dailyo.in/variety/case-pendency-litigation-supreme-court-judiciary-crpc-plea-bargaining/story/1/23908.html.

† Yash Agarwal, 'Why have Fast Track Courts Failed in India?', The Leaflet, 31 October 2020, https://www.theleaflet.in/why-have-fast-track-courts-failed-in-india/#.

‡ 'India Has Highest Bribery Rate In Asia: Transparency International', BQ Prime, 26 November 2020, https://www.bloombergquint.com/law-and-policy/india-has-highest-bribery-rate-in-asia-transparency-international.

places India highest with a bribery rate of 39 percent in Asia, wherein 45 percent of people had to use personal connections to get work done. Without a safe and confidential reporting mechanism, reigning rampant corruption is tough. Though India has fairly stringent anti-corruption laws like the Prevention of Corruption Act 1988, Foreign Contribution Regulation Act 2010, All India Services (conduct) Rules 1968, and Companies Act 2013, these laws must be aggressively implemented.

The problems that the SDGs attempt to tackle are too humongous and complex for government intervention alone. Several issues, such as health, water, and sanitation, are so intertwined that a siloed approach of a ministry, implementation challenges in program execution, and a complete absence of mechanisms for inter-ministerial or inter-institutional conversations and collaborations have left glaring gaps in the intended impact. A project-centric approach focused on achieving program targets fails to assess success on the ground. For instance, the Swachh Bharat Abhiyan undertook the large-scale building of toilets to stop open defecation. According to government reports, toilets have been built for around 92.7 million households, making 5,60,000 villages, 617 districts, and all thirty states open-defecation free.* Nevertheless, surveys of the same states reveal that toilet

---

* Christopher Finnigan, 'Has Modi's Swachh Bharat campaign been a success?', South Asia @ LSE, 16 May 2019, https://blogs.lse.ac.uk/southasia/2019/05/16/has-modis-swachh-bharat-campaign-been-a-success/#:~:text=Statistics%20on%20the%20government's%20official,30%20states%20open%2Ddefecation%20free.

construction has yet to be completed in many places. When completed, they did not have a water connection rendering them non-operational. In villages, rooms built for housing toilets were used as storage rooms, while obdurate villagers continued to defecate in the open.

Challenges impacting the case described above are gaps that non-governmental organizations have stepped in to fill. SCOPE, an NGO from Trichy led by Subbaraman,* its founder, identified contaminated water and consequent ill-health and medical expenses as the main reason for draining lower-income families' savings, keeping them in perpetual poverty. Subbaraman built over 20,000 toilets using an eco-friendly technology that could convert the septage into compost for farming. The NGO also offered bridge loans to poor households who needed more cash to construct a toilet, as the Swachh Bharat subsidy is transferred only after toilet construction.

Several companies have contributed their might to Swachh Bharat under the WASH segment.† ITC's Health and Sanitation Programme invested 105 crores in building low-cost sanitary units in twenty-two districts across fourteen states and mobilized

---

* 'SATO partners with NGOs to bring toilets to rural India', SATO, https://sato-p.dev-lixil.com/stories/sato-partners-with-ngos-to-bring-toilets-to-rural-india.
† 'A List of 10 big CSR Projects in WASH Sector in India (FY 2016-17)', CSRBOX, 23 March 2018, https://csrbox.org/India_CSR_news_A-List-of-10-big-CSR-Projects-in-WASH-Sector-in-India-(FY-2016-17)_291.

volunteers to educate villagers on their use. Power
Finance Corporation Limited focused on constructing
toilets in government schools, and so did NTPC and
ONGC under their Swachh Vidyalaya Abhiyan.

The government should work with the private
sector to evolve creative, cost-effective, and sustainable
solutions to our many socio-economic and ecological
problems. For instance, NITI Aayog is creating PPP
models that can bring in the latest technology, expertise,
and human resources to revamp the government's
lackluster afforestation program.[*] Similarly, large-
scale infrastructure development projects such as roads,
port development, eco-tourism, housing, and airport
projects that need substantial financial outlays are
other avenues that require collaborative efforts.[†] NITI
Aayog, as the fulcrum of cooperative federalism, works
on building strong Center-state, inter-government,
and inter-sectoral partnerships for accelerating India's
developmental agenda.[‡] In a participatory decision-
making process and government inclusion, non-state

---

[*] Sanya Dhingra, 'NITI Aayog plans private partnerships to revive
India's degraded forests', The Print, 27 August 2020, https://
theprint.in/environment/niti-aayog-plans-private-partnerships-to-
revive-indias-degraded-forests/488778/.

[†] 'Infra development through PPP to spur growth, create job;
Projects worth Rs 27,514 cr in FY20 till date', Economic Times,
2 February 2020, https://economictimes.indiatimes.com/news/
economy/indicators/infra-development-through-ppp-to-spur-
growth-create-job-projects-worth-rs-27514-cr-in-fy20-till-date/
articleshow/73866469.cms?from=mdr.

[‡] Niti Aayog, https://niti.gov.in/.

actors like corporates and civic society realize SDGs as a genuinely collective effort.

What can the corporate sector do?

No doubt, achieving SDGs needs the active participation of the private sector. Thanks to the global efforts that have gone into highlighting the role of the corporate players and making them part of cross-sector partnerships, there is a heightened awareness of SDGs among the corporate leadership. Many recognize that contributing to SDGs is strategically important and aim to do so in varied ways.

(1) *Corporate Social Responsibility Contributions to SDGs*

Many corporates find that aligning their CSR activities with SDGs is the easiest way to contribute to SDGs. With the amendment to the Companies Act 2013 through Section 135, companies' CSR contributions became mandatory rather than voluntary. Companies then began to draw out a CSR policy and articulated their CSR vision that went way beyond their business interests. Over the years, a pattern has emerged regarding the current social, livelihood, and environmental insufficiencies of companies that devote their CSR monies. Education (SDG 4) was the most popular sector for funding, followed by health and well-being (SDG 3) and poverty eradication (SDG 1). Peace, Justice and Strong Institutions (SDG 16), Sustainable Consumption and Production (SDG 12), and Life below Water (SDG 14) attracted the least investments.

It will be helpful for corporates to map their CSR activities against SDGs to understand for themselves where they stand (See the example at the end, of Tata Group CSR). This will further help them decide where they want to focus their energies and consolidate and deepen their CSR activities in ways that generate true social impact.

(2) *Corporate Social Innovations Advancing SDGs*

Corporations have also begun recognizing the interlinkages between their businesses and the SDGs. Many corporates' websites have now been modified to show which SDGs their businesses are helping to advance, directly or indirectly. While some opportunistically use it as mere PR, it is a more serious way to remind themselves and communicate to the stakeholders what their business stands for. They translate SDGs into corporate goals, set targets, initiate business and/or technology innovations to achieve the targets, track the progress diligently and make the results public.

> 'I did not have a market then, and I did not know where will I sell them. So all I did was to keep my staff occupied and help them survive.'
>
> —Priyanka Bapna, owner, Meemansa

Corporate Social Innovation is not the forte of large corporates alone. Micro, Small, and Medium-scale Enterprises (MSMEs) play a crucial role in socio-economic advancement through job creation and providing goods and services that reduce inequality and improve sustainable development. They are, therefore, critical contributors to SDG attainment. One example is Meemansa, a small-scale manufacturer of ready-to-wear garments in Mumbai. When Covid-19 halted business with few new orders, a market-aware and agile Meemansa switched to making protective face masks, the need of the hour. Using upcycled fabric, the team swiftly created design options that were comfortable to wear and trendy enough to appeal to differing tastes. A breakthrough was achieved when Meemansa approached IIT Bombay and licensed

---

SDGs fulfilled:

Ensuring Healthy Lives (SDG 3)
Employment and Decent work for all (SDG 8)
Empowering women and girls (SDG 5)
Fostering Innovation (SDG 9)

---

their Duraprot technology, a coating that crosslinks antibacterial and antiviral components onto the cloth. This enhanced their masks' health and safety quotient, making them effective and sought-after protection against Covid-19. The MSME thus commercialized a timely innovation and took it to the masses. Stitching masks provided livelihood to their employees who were stranded in the factory, unable to go home, and out of income as they were pieceworkers. Within a month, Meemansa, in collaboration with Helping Hands India, launched a Million Mask Challenge making masks available to those who could not afford them. The additional demand was met by training women who could stitch masks from their homes and earn an income during the lockdown. Meemansa grew from very modest beginnings to a 100-member stitching and manufacturing enterprise. One of the critical success factors for Meemnasa was its ability to develop a supply chain by tying up with wholesale buyers like TataCliq and Happy Masks. Currently, Meemnasa, in collaboration with Head Held High, is training women from self-help groups to set up similar manufacturing facilities, each capable of employing fifteen to twenty women, producing 10,000 to 20,000 masks per month. Meemansa has replicated its model in Gulbarga in Karnataka; Tonk, Chittor, and Udaipur in Rajasthan; Khajuraho in MP; Mumbai, Aurangabad, and Nagpur in Maharashtra; and Delhi—creating opportunities for livelihood and economic empowerment to over 200 women.*

(3) *SDGs Drive Social Enterprises*

Social enterprises—businesses that aim to generate profits to solve social and/or environmental problems— are well-placed to fasten our progress to achieving SDGs, given their inherent alignment. India is home to many social enterprises and is witnessing the emergence of more. Social enterprises work more directly with the social and environmental problems and devise solutions more tailored to the problems and the beneficiaries.

 Social enterprises can also help other organizations and entities in their efforts to support SDGs. They are seen to enter into partnerships with the government, NGOs, corporates,

---

* 'Interview With Manish Kothari', Fibre2Fashion, 14 December 2020, https://www.fibre2fashion.com/interviews/face2face/ meemansa/manish-kothari/12631-1/.

and other stakeholders. An example is Ecoparadigm, a Bengaluru-based boutique ecological engineering and consultancy firm poised to address environmental problems with minimalistic, resource-efficient, and sustainable solutions. The firm has consulted for the Ministry of Housing and Urban Affairs, Ministry of Urban Development, National Mission for Clean Ganga, International Council for Local Environment Initiatives (ICLEI), municipalities and nodal agencies assisting in policy building, awareness-raising, and consulting in the field of sustainable water and sanitation management. Ecoparadigm offers an example of a private firm aiding government waste and water management initiatives.

SDGs fulfilled:

Ensuring Healthy Lives (SDG 3)
Fostering Innovation (SDG 9)
Clean Water (SDG 6)
Clean Energy (SDG 7)

We conclude by underlining the need for a concerted effort among citizens, corporations, and enterprises of all sizes to partner with the government to ensure that we grow together robustly, righteously, and responsibly!

Annexure: Tata Group: An example for mapping CSR activities against SDGs

SDG Company	Project	Coverage
1	**No Poverty**	
Tata Global Beverage	Gaon Chalo Initiative for Rural Livelihood	70,000 villages, 18 states
Tata Power	Samridhi Programme for improving livelihoods of farmers	1,000 farmers (across 28 villages in Maval and Karjat talukas)
Tata Group	Tata Affirmative Action Programme	13,000 scholarships for students from the marginalized communities
Tata Steel	Improving Agricultural Productivity	Jharkhand and Odisha
2	**Zero Hunger**	
Rallis India Ltd.	Improving Livelihoods of Small and Marginal Farmers	Madhya Pradesh and Jharkhand
Tata Steel	Mission 2020 for Agriculture Development	Odisha
3	**Good Health and Well-Being**	
Tata Steel	Project Rishta	661 villages and 34 semi-urban slums from seven blocks of East Singhbhum and 305 villages from six blocks of Seraikela-Kharswan
Tata Motors	Combating Malnutrition	Jamshedpur, Jharkhand
Tata Steel	MANSI: Maternal and New-born Survival Initiative	Seraikela block of Seraikela-Kharswan district, Jharkhand
Tata International	Health Camps for a healthy future	Dewas, Madhya Pradesh
4	**Quality Education**	
Rallis India Ltd.	RUBY - Rallis Ujjwal Bhavishya Yojana	Maharashtra and Gujarat
Tata Communications	Together Towards a Digitally Inclusive Future	Bengaluru

	Jaguar Land Rover	Inspiring Tomorrow's Engineers: Tackling the Global STEM Skills Crisis	UK
	Tata Motors	Chance for Chasing Dreams	Puducherry, Mangalore
5		**Gender Equality**	
	Tata Steel	Empowering Girls Through Education	Jharkhand
	Tata Global Beverage	Empowering Women in India: Power of 49	All India realize
6		**Clean Water and Sanitation**	
	Tata Motors	Clean Water and Sanitation program	320 villages in Dharwad, Jamshedpur, Lucknow, Pantnagar, Pune, Sanand, and Thane
	Rallis India Ltd.	Model Tribal Village Development Project	Maharashtra, Gujarat
	TCS	Rain Water Harvesting Lakes	Chennai and Hyderabad
	TCS	Towards Creating Swachh Bharat	TCS Banyan Park, Mumbai.
	Titan	Watsan Project	Garhwal, Uttarakhand
	Tata Projects Business Unit	Gravity Flow Ultrafiltration for Safe Drinking Water for Tribals	Odisha
7		**Renewable Energy**	
	Tata Power	Demand-Side Management program	Mumbai
	Tata Power	Micro-Grid Solar Solutions	50 villages in the Tata Power neighborhood
8		**Decent Work and Economic Growth**	
	Tata Motors	Learn, Earn, and Progress (LEAP)	40 ITIs and 27 dealerships across the country
	Taj Hotels	Hospitality Skill Training Programme	Skill Training Centres in and around the regions of Taj Hotel operations
	Tata Housing	Samarth	across the nation

Tata Community Initiatives Trust	STRIVE Right Skills. Bright Future	Pune, Mohali, Mumbai, Aligarh, and Hyderabad
Tata Technologies	Ready Engineer Programme	tier 2 and 3 cities in India
Tata Chemicals	Livelihood Generation for Rural Women	Kenya (40 artisans), Lucknow (90 artisans), Babrala (30 artisans), Ahmedabad (20 artisans)
9	**Industry Innovation and Infrastructure**	
Rallis India Ltd.	Mission Jal Dhan and Jal Mitra	Kokan belt of Maharashtra
Voltas	Voltas Water Solutions (VWS)	GET.SET.RO., Sewage Treatment Plants
10	**Reduced Inequalities**	
Tata Teleservices Limited	Bridging the Divide: TEMA National Telecom Award; Mrs. Pilloo Dorab Khambatta Memorial Award * in partnership with the National Institute of the Visually Challenged	Uttar Pradesh
Tata Chemicals	Caring for Communities	Mithapur, Babrala, and Haldia
Tata Motors	Agricultural Development through Lift Irrigation	Kanikola and Jaskhandih, in Jamshedpur
Tata Power	Model Village Kadacimeth	Kadacimeth, Thane District, Maharashtra
11	**Sustainable Cities and Communities**	
Tata Housing	BIG: Beautiful is Green	Eco-friendly construction in India
12	**Responsible Consumption and Production**	
Taj Hotels	Driving Environmental Sustainability	Eight of its hotels were awarded Platinum Certifications, and 60 hotels received Gold Certification.

	Tata Steel	Including Sustainability Principles in New Product Development	Launched 32 new products, including new products for food and paint packaging, new types of tubes capable of withstanding extreme temperatures, and new products for the car and construction markets
	Tata Power	Promoting Sustainable Consumption through Societal Awareness	12 schools in Mumbai
	Tata Projects	Reutilisation of Waste Concrete Water	Nagarnar in Chhattisgarh
	Tata Chemicals	Integrated Approach to Water Management	Mithapur
13		**Climate Change**	
	TCS	Leading Low Carbon Growth	Green buildings, office infrastructure
	Tata Motors	Urgent Action to Combat Climate Change and its Impact	Mumbai Metropolitan Region Development Authority (MMRDA), Bandra-Kurla Complex, as well as for routes connecting BKC to the Airport
	Tata Motors	The Arrival of Zero Pollution Transportation	Developing a fleet of fuel-cell buses based on the hybrid platform series, which can provide clean public transportation in cities where hydrogen infrastructure will be available.
	Tata Steel	HISarna: Looking to the Future	Ijmuiden, Netherlands
14		**Life below Water**	
	Tata Chemicals	Save the Gentle Giants (Whale Sharks)	Gujarat

TCS	Marine Turtle Conservation Programme	Velas, Maharashtra
Tata Power	Saving the Mighty Mahseer	Walwhan, Lonavla
15	**Life on Land**	
Tata Global Beverages	Sustainable Beverages	Rainforest Alliance Certified™ farms for all their Tetley-branded teas in Europe, the Middle East, and Africa (EMEA) and Canada, America, and Australia
TCS	Butterfly Zones (butterfly conservation program)	Across 15 TCS locations
Tata International	Maintaining Environmental Sustainability	Dewas (Madhya Pradesh)
16	**Peace, Justice, and Strong Institutions**	
Tata group	All Institutions set up by the Tata Group	Tata Institute of Fundamental Research (TIFR), Indian Institute of Science (IISc), JRD Tata Ecotechnology Centre (JRDTEC), Tata Institute of Social Science, National Centre for Performing Arts (NCPA), Tata Medical Centre (TMC)
17	**Partnerships for the Goals**	
Tata Global Beverages	Rainforest Alliance	EMEA (Europe, the Middle East, and Africa) and CAA (Canada, Australia, and America) regions, Kanan Devan Hill Plantation (KDHP), Watawala in Sri Lanka
Tata Sustainability Group	Disaster Response Collaborating with partner organizations for relief and rehabilitation during humanitarian crises	India, Nepal

Sources:

https://www.tata.com/careers/affirmative-action

https://www.tatatrusts.org/upload/pdf/report-tata-group-and-the-sdgs.pdf

http://www.livolink.org/docs/Annual_Report_COMPP_2015-2016.pdf

https://www.rallis.co.in/DAR-2019-20/pdf/Business-Responsibility-Report.pdf

https://www.rallis.co.in/imagesInvestorRelations/effa4605-c3e8-4eac-83e9-91c793ad6a6c.pdf

https://www.pocketnewsalert.com/2015/07/Tata-Housing-to-provide-vocational-skill-development-training-to-100000-underprivileged-youth-by-2024.html

https://www.rallis.co.in/content.aspx?id=58&menuID=119

https://www.jbs.cam.ac.uk/wp-content/uploads/2020/08/report-wattr.pdf

https://www.ihcltata.com/content/dam/tajhotels/ihcl/sustainabilities/IHCL-Sustainability-Report-19.pdf

Part 2

Pathway 1—Corporate Social Responsibility

*'Businesses need to go beyond the interest of their
companies to the communities they serve.'*
*—Ratan Tata, Chairman Emeritus, Tata Industries,
Tata Motors,Tata Steel and Tata Chemicals*

3

Corporate Social Responsibility: Giving Back to Society

It is believed that the hands that rock the cradle build a nation. What would happen if those hands were emaciated and the cradle bereft of healthy babies?

Abhilash Yadav, a manager at Tata Steel Ltd in charge of CSR, was disturbed by a recent conversation with a local NGO. He discussed with community members and local NGOs to develop new project proposals for social development in the coming year. Recommendations had been developed based on pressing local needs that he could cull out of such conversations. Most of such requests involved problems with inadequate governmental resources or capabilities for a solution. One such issue was that of infant mortality. Preliminary need assessment reports highlighted that the hospitals in Seraikela-Kharswan (a district in Jharkhand) witnessed a disturbing rise in neonatal deaths. A record of 96 percent deaths during the neonatal stage in 2009 only underlined the newborns' abysmal health condition and their malnourished mothers. Investigations revealed low birth weight, asphyxia due to prolonged labor, and related infections like sepsis and pneumonia as the main culprits.

Early discussions with internal stakeholders led to the development of 'MANSI', a Maternal and Newborn Survival Initiative covering women from 167 villages from low-income families who had little access to maternal healthcare facilities. The initiative also aimed to train health workers to collect data on maternal health and inform and assist women in accessing medical facilities. With the correct and timely medical interventions, the program reduced the neonatal mortality rate (NMR) by 61 percent and Infant Mortality Rate (IMR) by 63 percent since its inception.

By 2014, MANSI became an example of a public-private partnership that brought together Tata Steel, the National Health Mission (NHM), American India Foundation (AIF), and the Society for Education Action and Research in Community Health (SEARCH), winning the Corporate Citizen of the Year 2014 ET award. The initiative has further enhanced the capabilities of government health volunteers (ASHAs/Sahiyas) in the Home-Based Newborn Care (HBNC) system reaching *out to over 58,620 pregnant women, mothers, and infants.*

~

The opening opportunity for a first-time manager aspiring to be an Impact Champion to contribute to the broader stakeholder community's betterment will likely be through Corporate Social Responsibility initiatives. Businesses have long since considered CSR as their way of giving back to society. By doing so, the organization is fulfilling its social obligation toward the societal stakeholders who have supported a business's setting up, survival, and growth by offering land, human resources, raw materials, and a market for products. This social obligation, in the past, was fuelled by patriotic feelings of helping a fledgling nation find its feet through industrialization and economic growth. Now, it has become a way for businesses to share the enormous developmental responsibility the government shoulders.

A brief history of corporate giving

Early instances of corporate giving in India date back to 1892 when Jamsetji Nusserwanji Tata set up the JN Tata Endowment fund to enable bright Indian students to study abroad. Later, Tata Iron & Steel Co Ltd was established, guided by the philosophy of corporate stewardship that valued social and community impact equally with operational performance. The interests of employees, customers, and the nation itself were regarded as necessary along with those of the corporate. Several others, too, contributed in the form of charity, as prescribed by a religion or encouraged by social customs.

During the pre-independence period, Gandhiji advocated the trusteeship approach. The trusteeship approach's basic premise was that the rich were merely the custodians of the wealth they generated as the resources with which they generated wealth belonged to society. Hence, they had the responsibility of sharing it with the community for its socio-economic upliftment.[*]

Post-Independence, the mantel of social responsibility fell on the public sector organizations, who continue to be the most significant contributor to CSR efforts.[†] Public sector organizations have contributed to nation-building by setting up offices, factories, and townships in remote and underdeveloped places while offering employees a fulfilling work environment and healthcare facilities.

Liberalization, privatization, and globalization that brought in impressive growth for private sector

---

[*] 150 Years of Celebrating the Mahatma, https://gandhi.gov.in/social-responsibility.html#:~:text=Mahatma%20Gandhi%20believed%20in%20the,communities%20and%20the%20natural%20environment.

[†] Samrat Sharma, 'PSUs outshine private firms as India Inc pushes CSR funds to fight coronavirus; check top contributors', *Financial Express*, 10 June 2020, https://www.financialexpress.com/economy/psus-outshine-private-firms-as-india-inc-pushes-csr-funds-to-fight-coronavirus-check-top-contributors/1986974/.

companies also required them to be conscious of their actions' social and environmental impact to ensure sustainability. As a result, acceptable business practices like stakeholder engagement and community relationship management, ecological consciousness, responsible sourcing, diversity and inclusiveness, and transparency in governance became the norm.

In 2011, the Indian government endorsed the United Nations Guiding Principles on Business and Human Rights. Following this, the National Voluntary Guidelines on social, environmental, and economic responsibilities of business were issued the same year, stating upfront the government's expectations of conduct from corporations. Developed after extensive consultations with varied stakeholder groups, these guidelines nudged enterprises across all sectors and different sizes, including multinational corporations, to harmonize profitability with human development and adequate environmental safeguards. The guidelines proposed that enterprises ensure responsible business practices within their factories and extend them to their value chain partners and the broader ecosystem in which they undertook their business.

Nine Principles of Responsible Business Practices

1. Conduct business with ethics, transparency, and accountability

2. Manufacture and sell goods and services that are safe and sustainable
3. Ensure the well-being of all employees
4. Be respectful and responsive towards all stakeholders, especially the disadvantaged, vulnerable, and marginalized
5. Respect and promote human rights
6. Respect, protect, and preserve the environment
7. Be responsible when influencing public and regulatory policy
8. Safeguard inclusive growth and equitable development
9. Be accountable and offer value to customers and consumers

The NVG successfully communicated to the industry the need to combine financial metrics with several non-financial measures for assessing performance. However, its limitation was its voluntary nature and a need for more credible information on the extent to which corporations adopted the guidelines.

The Indian government soon felt significant resources could be garnered from companies for social development. This prompted an amendment to Section 135 in the Companies Act of 2013, making India the only country to mandate corporate social responsibility.* This legislation changed corporate giving for social development from voluntary contribution to compliance.

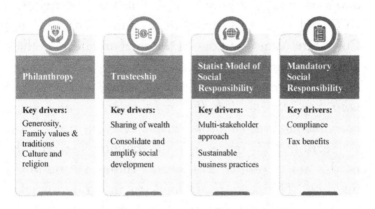

Figure 1: Evolution of Social Responsibility in India

Nudging corporates to contribute

Now let us see how social responsibility became mandatory compliance. After decades of giving the industry the freedom to decide on the quantum and mode of contribution to social causes, the government amended Section 135 of the Companies Act. The amendment's objective was to formalize corporate giving to a broader stakeholder base and set benchmarks for the contributions from all companies

---

* Priya Nair Rajeev and Suresh Kalagnanam, 'India's mandatory CSR policy: implications and implementation challenges', *International Journal of Business Governance and Ethics* 12.1 (2017): 90–106.

that made profits. These changes were featured in the amendment to Section 135 of the Companies Act in 2013, considered a turning point in India's developmental trajectory. Dr. Bhaskar Chatterjee, CEO and Director General of the Indian Institute of Corporate Affairs and one of the chief architects of the amendment, stated that *Section 135 is the culmination of many years of thought, consultation, and debates with key stakeholders like corporates, government, parliamentarians, civil society, and NGOs.*

Section 135 represents the country's essential needs and co-opts corporate India in nation-building. The section attempts to integrate social, economic, and environmental concerns in companies' choices, decisions, and actions in managing their stakeholders. Such an integrated effort will help redirect organizational attention and efforts toward sustaining the triple bottom line—profits, people, and the planet. As a first-time manager, you will benefit from understanding the critical constituents of Section 135 that specify corporate inclusion and responsibility through four key dimensions, as indicated in Figure 2.

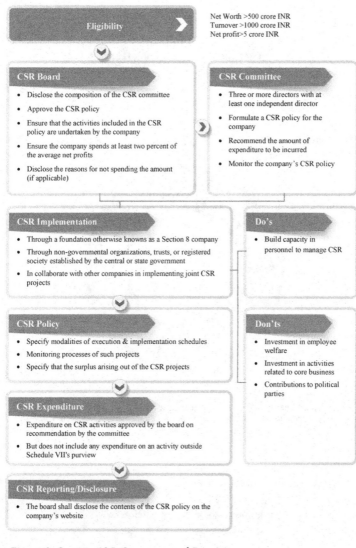

Figure 2: Section 135: Structure and Provisions

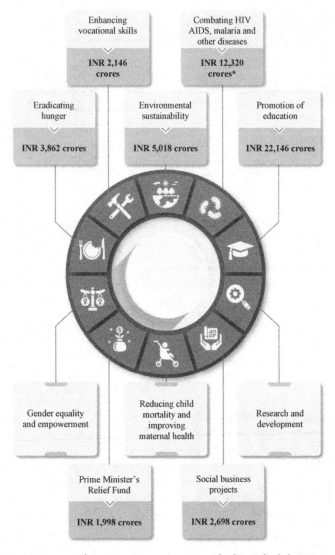

Figure 3: Areas of CSR investment as prescribed in Schedule VII

CSR investments mentioned are from 2014–19. *Some figures may include more than one area of investment (e.g. healthcare includes maternal health)

How effective has Section 135 been in augmenting social investments?

Undoubtedly, the government's objective to bring in more funds in under-invested areas of social infrastructure like education and healthcare has received a boost. Data indicates that corporations have mostly responded positively to the amendment, investing INR 72,000 crore between 2014 and 2019. This developmental funding by 29,000 corporates in CSR makes it a primary source of social sector investment for the government. Among the significant areas of investment, education sector is the foremost, followed by health care and rural development, with CSR monies being spent countrywide. The banking

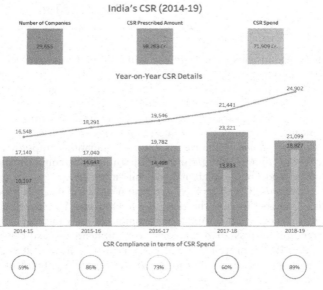

and financial services sector made the most extensive contributions.

There has been a 50 percent increase between 2014 and 2019 in the number of companies under the purview of Section 135 and an increase in spending by 85 percent during the same period. This is a very positive sign, indicating greater compliance from corporations. CSR Compliance in terms of CSR spending with regard to the prescribed amount in 2018–19 has been the highest at 89 percent since the mandating of CSR.*

> 'The clichéd two percent regime doesn't really mean anything to us in terms of a mathematical calculation. Our model of CSR goes beyond Schedule 7.'
>
> —Sourav Roy,
> Head CSR Tata Steel

---

* IndiaDataInsights data from the Ministry of Corporate Affairs portal, March 2020.

'Tata Steel felicitates women health volunteers for project MANSI', Press Release, Tata Steel, 27 March 2018, https://www.tatasteel.com/media/newsroom/press-releases/india/2018/tata-steel-felicitates-women-health-volunteers-for-project-mansi/.

'Clinton Global Initiative', Clinton Foundation, https://www.clintonfoundation.org/clinton-global-initiative/commitments/mansi-model-reduce-maternal-and-child-mortality.

'ET Awards 2014: Tata Steel's commitment to social causes makes it Corporate Citizen of the Year', *Economic Times*, 1 October 2014, https://economictimes.indiatimes.com/news/company/corporate-trends/et-awards-2014-tata-steels-commitment-to-social-causes-makes-it-corporate-citizen-of-the-year/articleshow/43961029.cms?utm_source=contentofinterest&utm_medium=text&utm_campaign=cppst.

By 2018–19, of the total 15,064 reporting companies, 39 percent spent more than the prescribed CSR while only 25 percent spent less than the prescribed CSR. These figures are a clear indication of the fact that companies appreciate the need to contribute to social development. The PM-CARES fund received around Rs 2,105 crore from thirty-eight public sector undertakings, apparently from CSR funds for 2019–20 that could not be utilized. Delays in implementation, delays in getting regulatory clearances, exploring opportunities, and investment in long-term projects are the main reasons for the underutilization of funds. A 100 percent tax exemption exists for Prime Minister's fund contributions.

Though the amendment is touted as a *bold experiment*, the government has been careful not to force social responsibility through punitive measures. For example, there are no penalties for those who fail to spend 2 percent of their net profits on socially responsible interventions.

How do you implement CSR projects?

As a first-time manager, it will be helpful to understand how these investment decisions are made. Recently, CSR investment choices have become very data-driven, with information on the pattern of spending and area-specific needs getting priority in project choice and budget allocation. Public sector organizations continued to be the flagbearers of social investments between 2014–19 and contributed 56 percent of CSR spending. While private limited companies comprising 62 percent of participants in CSR contributed 19 percent of CSR spent during the same period. We shall now look at some critical elements a new manager needs to appreciate about the administration of social responsibility projects.

- *Role of the CSR Board*

Wisely investing 2 percent of a company's net profit is an onerous responsibility of the CSR Board, which must draft a well-thought-out action plan. Section 135 has a few recommendations on the implementation of social responsibility initiatives as well. The Board recommends budgetary provisions for the social responsibility projects and periodically monitors the progress and performance of the above. The Board comprising at least three or more directors, of which one needs to be an independent director, is responsible for publishing the CSR policy on the company's website. They will need to specify the reasons the company cannot spend the allocated CSR budget in a given financial year.

- *Modes of Implementation*

Appreciating the fact that all companies need not have the administrative capability to execute social responsibility projects internally, Section 135 offers corporations FOUR different means of implementing CSR projects:

1. Undertake CSR projects through a foundation, otherwise known as a Section 8 company set up exclusively by a company (e.g., Infosys Foundation) or a collaborative effort with any other company.

2. Partner with non-governmental organizations or a trust or registered society established by the Central or state government with a proven track record of three years in commissioning similar projects to be selected as an implementation partner. (e.g., ITC and Pratham together in the Reach India Plus initiative).

3. Collaborate with other companies in implementing joint CSR projects by pooling in resources and thereby expanding the scope and impact of the project (e.g., Mphasis and Uber launched Uber Assist and Uber Access, which retro-fitted vehicles to help Persons with Disabilities as their joint CSR initiative).

4. Do it internally by developing the capabilities of their employees as CSR managers as well as training the staff of the partner NGO (e.g., Calpine Technologies CSR program Engage undertaken by their employees)

CSR implementation through corporate foundations and employee volunteering have been popular routes adopted. The two examples below illustrate their varied advantages and outcomes.

Employee engagement for and through CSR

Cognizant Outreach is a global CSR initiative launched by Cognizant in 2007 to commemorate achieving its second billion-dollar revenue mark by supporting its stakeholders. Made up entirely of Cognizant associates/employee volunteers and company funding, Outreach seeks to alleviate inequalities in access to education due to socio-economic backwardness, gender inequalities, and lack of facilities in remote villages. The pathway they chose to alleviate disparities in educational access was by using video conferencing to connect students from remote villages and prepare them to compete for opportunities and resources in a highly competitive world. Company sources report that Outreach volunteers teach nearly 100 classroom sessions in India weekly using innovative teaching methods that have helped several partnering schools record a 100 percent pass percentage in class X and XII board examinations. Visually challenged students were assisted in learning effectively with recorded audiobooks, and employee volunteers designed regular learning sessions for students with learning disabilities. In addition, the Career Awareness sessions have helped around 150,000 students make informed career choices. Since 2012, the Outreach Scholarship Program has supported over 2,110 students based on merit, 72 percent being girls. Over 90 percent of these scholars are first-time graduates who have since found employment in companies, including Cognizant.

Now a part of the Self4society initiative launched in 2019, Outreach has around 50,000 active volunteers in India. Their volunteering efforts support educating and skilling students, improving digital literacy, and helping the differently-abled and opportunity-deprived. Since its inception, employees have cumulatively devoted over 3.1 million hours to volunteering, positively impacting over 700,000 lives. In addition, the program has spread its wing to cover other areas, including community welfare and environmental sustainability.

The critical success factor of Outreach is its grassroots-level community service led by employee volunteers. Grassroots-level engagements have benefited the community immensely and have brought about positive organizational outcomes like greater job satisfaction, reduced stress, and a strong sense of identification with and pride in the company. 'Several employees have said they would prefer to stay with Cognizant due to the tangible difference Outreach has made to their life,' says Archana Raghuram, program manager of Cognizant Outreach.

Foundation as a vehicle of CSR

SBI Foundation is the CSR wing of the State Bank of India, which works by creating inclusive and sustainable development through ethical behavior. Their focal areas include healthcare and sanitation, education, livelihood, skill development, women empowerment and care for senior citizens, sustainability and environment, and rural development. Of the Foundation's several programs, Youth for India is unique in its focus, structure, and implementation. The premise of YFI is that 'every village has the necessary capacities to develop themselves sustainably, and change can be initiated using the skill sets of urban Indian youth to catalyze rural development.'

One of the YFI Fellows, Mehak Aggarwal, like any other technical graduate from an upper-middle-class family, joined Infosys, Bengaluru, a dream company for many techies like her. Soon 'I was bored with my job at Infosys and knew that I needed something stimulating and meaningful.' The Fellowship provides opportunities for the more privileged sections to become aware of ground realities and contribute through their efforts to build healthy, cohesive communities; and inculcate a spirit of social entrepreneurship.

The Fellowship operates in three phases—familiarization, implementation, and sustenance.

During the week-long orientation, YFI fellows are given an introductory perspective and an overview of rural development. An NGO assigns a location, domain, and local mentor who helps the Fellow interact with stakeholders from the community and local authorities to understand pressing issues that need solutions. Mehak Aggarwal recounts, 'I was assigned to BAIF, Pune, and my location was Shahpur block in Betul district, Madhya Pradesh. It was a tribal block, and my life took a 180-degree turn from my Bangalore days, but in a good way.' The NGO and SBI YFI approve the intervention and implementation plan once it is ready, giving the Fellow a nine-month timeframe for implementation. In the sustenance phase, the Fellow must identify a person from the local community or NGO who could take over and continue the project.

The program started in 2011 with an initial batch of twenty-seven fellows and currently has fifty-two fellows working at thirty-five rural locations across twelve states of India. Three hundred and three alumni work in diverse fields, with 70 percent working in the development sector. An exemplar of YFI is Sanjana Yadav, a fellow for the year 2017–18 who, with the help of teachers, NGO volunteers, and local communities, developed and integrated a gender-sensitive curriculum in schools in Tilolia, Rajasthan. Sanjana used poster-making, storytelling, poetry recitals, debates, skits, and group activities to engage students and sensitize them on gender issues, domestic violence, child marriage, stereotypes, and menstruation. This curriculum is used in fifty-seven schools and colleges and piloted in twenty NTPC locations across eleven states. Sanjana's efforts and contribution were recognized by UN Volunteers India when she was bestowed the V-Award, in 2018.

Convinced of its ground-breaking potential, Mr. Nixon Joseph, President and COO of SBI Foundation, asserts that 'this is a movement that can transform India's best young minds, especially socially motivated youth, into changemakers. The fellowship has developed a trusted gateway for higher talents to flow into rural development, thereby reviving the grassroots development machinery for benefiting marginalized communities.' The impact of this program is assessed using performance matrixes that capture the increase in the number of girls attending school compared to the previous year, the rise in employment secured by villagers, and the extent of empowerment and self-reliance attained by women, to name a few.

The partnerships forged between corporates and NGOs (referred to as other implementing agencies in the figure below) have not been limited to project implementation but begin with need assessment and program design. Additionally, companies directly implementing CSR projects assist NGOs in program design, on-the-ground implementation monitoring, evaluation, and impact assessment.

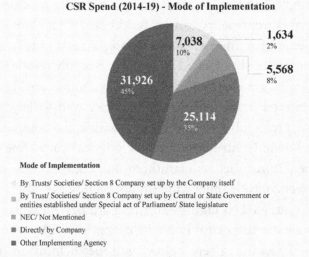

CSR Spend (2014-19) - Mode of Implementation

Mode of Implementation

By Trusts/ Societies/ Section 8 Company set up by the Company itself

By Trust/ Societies/ Section 8 Company set up by Central or State Government or entities established under Special act of Parliament/ State legislature

NEC/ Not Mentioned

Directly by Company

Other Implementing Agency

@ IndiaDataInsights.com | Notes: Data as updated on MCA portal as of Mar 2020

• *Invest in Long-Term Impactful Projects*

One of the main objectives of mandating CSR was to inspire companies to invest in long-term projects that are likely to be impactful. However, implementing social responsibility projects has been challenging for corporates uninitiated in social development work. Therefore, companies need to develop a well-thought-out CSR strategy that identifies local developmental needs and seeks to address them. One-off or intermittent projects undertaken to spend the allocated funds may not offer developmental outcomes.

Further, companies are advised to avoid picking up CSR projects in line with their core business. For example, priority sector lending by banks to women micro-entrepreneurs cannot be deemed CSR. Nor can activities that improve the workforce's quality of life and their families be clubbed under CSR. Socially responsible activities are meant for the socio-economic well-being of external stakeholders, communities, and society and must preferably be implemented within the company's local area. Contributions to any political party, one-off expenditures such as marathons and competitions, and projects outside India will also not qualify as CSR.

You need to take several preparatory measures to ensure the successful implementation of CSR projects. The checklist given below will be helpful in the groundwork:

Checklist for implementation CSR for companies

1. Train CSR committee members in designing and implementing CSR projects.
2. Include an independent director in the CSR board for better governance.
3. Develop a comprehensive CSR policy stating the company's CSR mission and vision, strategic focus, and operating guidelines

4. Develop clear guidelines, set predetermined criteria, perform due diligence, and identify suitable NGOs to implement CSR activities.

5. Keep administrative expenses of CSR projects within the allowed 5 percent of the annual CSR outlay.

6. Develop reporting mechanisms in compliance with the prescribed reporting format.

7. Gain clarity on accounting challenges like treating expenses as CSR expenses, funds committed but not incurred on CSR, and internal audit of CSR expenses.

8. Develop a structured approach to measuring the social impact of CSR projects undertaken.

- *Choosing an NGO Partner*

While the Act offers the option of setting up a trust or Section 8 company to manage corporate CSR, it suggests working with NGOs for smaller organizations. As a result, several companies new to CSR opt to find a like-minded NGO partner. However, choosing an implementation partner is one of the most vexing issues corporates face. While selecting an NGO partner, companies have found a staggering number of choices. A CBI report submitted to the Supreme Court (Mahapatra, 2014) estimated that approximately 20 lakh NGOs currently operate in the country. Some studies put the figure at 30 lakh, one NGO for every 400 citizens, twice the number of schools, and 250 times the number of government hospitals. Nevertheless, sifting through such numbers, choosing the right NGO partner, and building a working relationship can be challenging in the absence of a reliable NGO rating system.

CRISIL announced an NGO evaluation process in 2014, which grades NGOs based on their performance and financial proficiency. However, grading NGOs has been challenging as several fail to file audit reports with the authorities periodically and need more efficient and transparent processes to govern them. In such a scenario, you must remember that several specific criteria can aid in an apt selection. We list them below:

Checklist for selecting an NGO partner

1. Look at the nature of the NGO's past program and speak to some of the stakeholders and beneficiaries for an assessment.
2. Check if the NGO has worked in contexts where the CSR project will be implemented.
3. Enquire about the grassroots connect of the NGO volunteers in the local area of the project.
4. Assess the skills and competencies of the volunteers as well as their average tenure in the organization.

5. Ensure they have been in operation for at least three years.
6. Find out about the nature of their funders to assess their financial stability. For example, do they have a few big donors or several small ones? What are their credentials?

• *Reporting CSR Initiatives*

CSR reporting has significant diversity, perhaps resulting from factors such as the motivation to disclose, the industry(ies) within which an individual company operates, the diversity of stakeholders, and company size. Though we see an increase in CSR spend, the framing of clear CSR policies has yet to be completed by several companies or, if completed, has not been shared on the company website as required under Section 135. The MCA data (March 2020) evidences that the CSR policies of almost 62 percent of eligible companies have yet to be made public even while the section mandates making available the annual CSR report.

• *Assessing the Impact of CSR*

While issues regarding the implementation of CSR projects are still being sorted out, what stands out as the next crucial item on the CSR agenda is the assessment of social return on investment. We cannot assess progress and changes in the local contexts without a robust measurement mechanism and regular project implementation reviews.

Anecdotal evidence points to many corporates measuring outcomes reported on the company websites rather than assessing the impact of such projects. The next step in advancing social responsibility would be developing social indicators to measure sustainability and incorporate them as measures of success.

4

Social Impact Assessment: A Key Tool to Ensure Real Impact

Asha Chauhan was busy preparing a new CSR project proposal to be implemented in the upcoming fiscal year. Just then, her boss, the head of CSR at AXC Foundation, the CSR arm of AXC company, inquired about the impact assessment report of a recently completed skill development project. Asha had been somewhat unhappy with the third-party assessment report of the same. While the report highlighted outcomes, there was nothing much to show in terms of actual change they could bring about in people's lives. Moreover, the assessment report posed a problem as the project had begun with many expectations of change. While the skill development program covered over 200 school dropouts, there needed to be more information on how the newly acquired skills helped establish a livelihood for the beneficiaries.

What should be the metrics to assess social impact? When is the right time to evaluate? Asha needed to get back to the drawing board on their social responsibility initiatives and decide which point of the development continuum the company should invest in. So she decided to spend the next few days researching social impact assessment to answer her many questions on what makes a CSR investment worthwhile.

AXC Foundation had chosen to invest in education as an essential investment into the future of the next generation, capable of offering knowledge, skills, and attitudes that prepare a student for a profession while providing a route out of poverty for the family and improving the socio-economic outcomes for the community. This 'ripple effect' demonstrates the broad socio-economic impact a program can bring.

~

Corporations view CSR as a unique opportunity to make a significant social impact, especially on the lives of local communities, the underprivileged, the poor, and the marginalized. On a cursory glance at the annual list of the Top 20 Indian Companies for CSR,* most of them have developed elaborate frameworks to guide

---

* 'Top Indian companies for CSR in 2019', CSR Journal, https://thecsrjournal.in/top-indian-companies-for-csr-2019/.

their social responsibility projects that span community development, drinking water and sanitation, healthcare, education, farming and livelihood, sports and culture, and environmental protection and restoration. With over Rs 11,392 crore spent by eligible companies in FY 2018–19 and a generous helping hand offered in cash and kind to combat the pandemic,* corporate altruism is rising. However, how do we know if these activities make an impact? What is the nature of the impact they have on people and the planet? How much do they contribute to achieving the Sustainable Development Goals (SDGs)?

This is not a question for CSR projects alone. Corporate Social Innovations and Social Enterprises must also answer these questions to claim they generate true social impact. While it is evident that Social Innovations and Social Enterprises are tailored solutions for specific social and environmental problems, it is not straightforward to establish if and to what extent they have helped solve the problem. For example, the World Health Organization (WHO) has classified India as hyper-endemic for dengue, meaning that the virus is active throughout the country most of the year. The monsoon and winter months are the worst. However, several rural healthcare centers need more basic testing facilities, delaying, if not

---

* 'India CSR reporting survey 2019', KPMG, February 2020, https://assets.kpmg.com/content/dam/kpmg/in/pdf/2020/02/india-s-csr-reporting-survey-2019.pdf.

denying, timely treatment. Dr. Rashbehari and Dr. Binita Tunga, a husband-and-wife team, devised an alternative solution, innovating a diagnostic device capable of successfully detecting malaria, dengue, and chikungunya within ten minutes on the first day of showing symptoms of the disease. More promising is that their testing kit requires no specific equipment or trained technicians to deploy. Their social enterprise, Ameliorate Bio-Tech, combines a social innovation (an antigen-based kit for chikungunya that does not need any equipment) and a business model (a novel platform technology to manufacture and market diagnostic kits) that reaches the BoP population at INR 600 whereas competing test kits sell for INR 5,000. How do they discover the impact their innovation and business model have on preventing and treating these diseases?

Why measure social impact?

Although the amount of money and energy invested in CSR, Corporate Social Innovation, and Social Enterprises are going up yearly, ensuring that they deliver actual social impact has taken a backseat. Since the government moved social responsibility from being a gesture of charity to a mandated duty by Section 135 of The Companies Act 2013, social impact assessment has become a much-discussed topic. Nevertheless, in the ten years of mandatory CSR, most companies have yet to progress from merely reporting their CSR activities. Many report the amounts they have spent or outcomes, such as the number of additional rooms built in a rural hospital and a list of equipment they bought, but very few robustly assess the impact.

It is absurd if a company spends a substantial amount of money on a marketing campaign and then does not measure the sales. But, then, would not assessing social impact be absurd, having made significant investments? We highlight this as an aspect that Impact Champions should pay close attention to.

Measuring social impact would help the Impact Champions answer the following questions: Are the initiatives they have launched—CSR, CSI, or Social Entrepreneurship—generating the societal benefit they promise? Are they bringing about the changes that they had envisioned? Can they improve their reach? How can the impact be enhanced?

Answers to these questions help in various ways.

- Once the project is completed, an impact assessment helps compare the realized outcomes with the intentions, and any discrepancy can be addressed. This information helps improve the conceptualization, detailing, and execution of future projects. In addition, assessments offer valuable feedback that the Impact Champions can use to make project execution more strategic and effective.

- Measuring a project's social impact has become increasingly important for companies to make an informed choice of investment among various alternatives available, in line with their vision. Since companies must allocate their scarce resources among compelling and often competing requirements, such an assessment is critical for ensuring the most effective spending. It will help the Impact Champions be more persuasive in garnering support for their initiatives.

- A report card of the social responsibility projects is essential for reporting to stakeholders and assessing return on investment and as an input for future investment decisions. Impact assessment reports are credible sources that can be shared with stakeholders and the general public as a statement of social value addition contributed by the organization.

- Impact assessment makes the CSR department, partner NGO and other stakeholders accountable for their deliverables and ensures that the project is professionally managed. Furthermore, undertaking an evaluation gives the assessor a chance to seek candid feedback from stakeholders about their project experiences and suggestions for improvement. In most social projects, that is the only opportunity of getting more comprehensive feedback on the social value of initiatives.

Equally, not doing an impact assessment can be damaging to the cause. Making sure that actual impact is made takes effort. There is a distressing tendency among many corporates to engage in token activities that will get them good PR (e.g., donating money to hospitals or distributing uniforms to poor students) rather than pursue real impact (e.g., measuring health outcomes for the patients in that hospital or improvement in the educational attainment of the students). If you are an Impact Champion, who is serious about what you do, this is something that you will have to guard against. Having a robust impact assessment plan will be of paramount importance to you.

The above needs a tool for critical examination of the on-the-ground realities that can report back on successes and point to areas that need improvement. Social Impact Assessment (SIA) is one such tool. In this chapter, we introduce you to the concept and implementation of SIA. We will explain the nuances of undertaking SIA to measure and track social impact and fill the gaps. SIA can be applied to track impact in any pathway you use—CSR, CSI, or Social Entrepreneurship. For example, in the CSR space, SIA will be a valuable tool to assess how successful BPCL's Project Boondh has been using rainwater harvesting to augment water availability and improve the water table in over 200 water-deficient villages across six states. SIA can gauge the extent to which a social innovation like Neurosynaptic Communications, a medical devices company, has improved healthcare access for the rural poor through telemedicine facilities that enable faster diagnosis and appropriate treatment from expert doctors. Impact assessment can estimate the improvement in student learning outcomes for Megashala, a social enterprise that empowers teachers with instructional resources, thereby improving teaching quality. We illustrate with examples of how to undertake such evaluations.

Figure 1: Interventions assessed using SIA

Social Impact Assessment: What is it?

Social impact assessment (SIA) is a systematic approach for assessing (in advance or post-facto) the social and economic consequences of CSR projects, Corporate Social Innovations, or Social Enterprises. It includes an all-encompassing framework for reviewing and evaluating the social effects of activities and interventions implemented under the programs. Therefore, SIA focuses on 'the triple bottom line' (Elkington, 1997), comprising a project's economic, community, and environmental performances over time.

SIA entails adopting a proactive stance for continually improving the project's developmental outcomes, nudging companies to make their social investments choice more systematic. They may consult their CSR mission and objectives while designing projects, gathering baseline data, and developing metrics for monitoring and evaluation rather than just spending monies to meet mandatory targets. CSR investments are usually made for improving human capital (e.g., ICICI Academy for Skills), protecting the environment (e.g., Northern Coalfields Limited Swaksh Jal project that built two check dams), as well as better managing stakeholder relationships (e.g., Integrated Village Development near Kudgi by Power Grid Corporation). Therefore, the appraisal needs to be robust. In the case of social enterprises, particularly those that have received funding from impact investors, assessments must incorporate investment appraisals (which assess an investment's profitability, affordability, and strategic fit to the organization) and stakeholder evaluation (the measurement of outcomes for stakeholders). A comprehensive SIA includes both.

Let us understand investment appraisal and stakeholder evaluation examples. Climate change is one of the most disturbing phenomena that has affected several aspects of our daily lives. Asia, in general, and India, in particular, have borne the brunt of unforgiving droughts, unseasonal rains, and flash floods. Climate changes, particularly water scarcity, have assaulted agriculture, the most vital sector. CultYvate is a precision Ag Tech company that aims to enhance agriculture productivity. Their objective is to increase crop yield while reducing farm inputs with precision farming technology built on climate-predicting technology. They also advise on water and soil conservation, reducing carbon footprint by offering aggregation solutions, storage, and optimizing the supply chain management route. The company is funded by Villgro, a pioneering social enterprise incubator. Continually assessing a start-up's growth and performance is critical for Villgro to alleviate poverty by scaling social impact. Despite holding much promise, impact investors are not enthusiastic about supporting Ag Tech companies. 'Unfortunately, investors do not understand technologies. They cannot understand how to value the company, how it should scale, and their business model. Thus, investors end up giving it a pass,' says Srinivas Ramanujam, CEO of Villgro.* Impact assessment would generate data for investor evaluations, easing more investments into social innovations.

Similarly, social enterprises need continuous stakeholder appraisal to improve their product and scale. Meghshala was the fruit of Jyothi Thyagarajan's dream to enhance education quality made available to thousands of children in government schools. However, improvements were possible only if teachers had the resources and skills to teach better. Meghshala offered a solution that helped empower and upskill teachers through best-in-class teaching kits and teacher mentoring and guidance for performance enhancement, benefiting thousands of students through 4,500 lessons in English and vernacular languages in 2,500 schools. Meghshala commissioned a qualitative impact assessment study by a third party, Gray Matters India. In the first three years, the purpose was to understand student learning outcomes through assessments. Post student testing, they analyzed teachers' behavioral patterns. This analysis helped develop customized student experiences through better teacher training and mentoring to improve teaching styles. Stakeholder assessment thus provided necessary inputs for product up-gradation.

---

* Amit Raja Naik, 'Impact Incubator Villgro On Two Decades Of Backing India's Agritech Ecosystem', Inc42, 21 October 2020, https://inc42.com/features/impact-incubator-villgro-on-two-decades-of-backing-indias-agritech-startups/.

Is SIA mandatory?

In India, government-mandated SIA has featured only in the laws related to land acquisition for projects. SIA appears in The Right to Fair Compensation and Transparency in Land Acquisition, Rehabilitation and Resettlement Act (2013). All significant projects under the purview of the two acts need to conduct an SIA within six months of the project's start date. Here the Act ensures that stakeholder unrest and protests by affected parties do not erupt, and the implementing company can avoid any potential harm to them in project execution. SIA is a proactive study that assesses the possible consequences of projects on people, communities, and the environment.

In the context of CSR, Section 135 of the Companies Act 2013, Rule 5 (2) requires the CSR committee to create a transparent monitoring mechanism while implementing CSR projects or programs. The CSR committee is also entrusted with auditing the projects' accounts and appointing a competent third party to assess the impact of the CSR projects. Impact assessment is, however, still a 'nice to have', not mandatory. It is a bit different for PSUs. In addition to the provisions of Section 135, the Department of Public Enterprises (DPE) has framed CSR and Sustainability Guidelines for all Central public sector enterprises. The guidelines require the public sector to monitor their CSR projects by a CSR committee, a social audit committee, or an appropriate credible external agency. On completion, projects are to be evaluated by a suitable external agency. The purpose of the evaluation is to assess the project's social impact; the number of beneficiaries whose life has been enhanced by the socio-economic value-adds the CSR project has brought about. Therefore, a meaningful impact assessment requires a detailed evaluation design that can help define evaluation parameters and pick the right tools to capture the extent of the benefit accrued.

How does the nature of the project matter in SIA?

We can differentiate social projects in terms of their target beneficiaries. Some projects

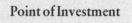

Point of Investment

have micro-level beneficiaries (e.g., scholarships for academically brilliant students), while others offer interventions for improving school administration, creating a meso-level benefit. Companies can choose to invest in different points of the benefit continuum, for example, in education, ranging from donations to setting up training schools. The moot point is to understand that while investment at each level is essential, they differ in the impact they can create. Some offer immediate benefits, and few others leave a more long-lasting imprint. The impact assessment metrics would be different in each case.

I. **Donations** (in cash or kind as in tables, chairs, computers, accessories, etc.)

 UltraTech Community Welfare Foundation, through Shala Praveshotsav, the school enrolment campaign, has supported over 40,200 students by providing notebooks, school bags, and uniforms.

II. **Teaching students** (extra lessons in maths, languages, computer science, career counseling, etc., using employee volunteering)

 Tata Power's Educational Excellence Program, in association with PRATHAM, offers employee volunteers a chance to coach students in English and Maths remotely in Tiruldih, Jharkhand.

III. **Improving attendance at schools** (transport arrangements to reach schools, building hostels)

 Power Grid Corporation of India Ltd built a boys' hostel for Pt. Ravishankar Shukla University (Chhattisgarh), provided a school bus to government primary and secondary schools, improving access to schools for children in far-flung Murbari (Assam).

IV. **Enabling students to access education** (scholarships to students for higher studies)

 Wipro has supported and enabled more than 30,000 students to pursue higher education in engineering with India's premier engineering institutions under the programs WASE, WiSTA, and WIMS. As a result, over 18,200 students completed their M.Tech degrees in various IT disciplines over the last two decades.

V. **Improving school infrastructure** (refurbishing classrooms, building new toilets, science laboratory)

 Northern Coalfields Limited works extensively towards developing the necessary infrastructure of government primary, middle, and high schools and anganwadis in the villages and improving the quality of education through SMART classes in Singrauli (Madhya Pradesh) and Sonbhadra (Uttar Pradesh).

VI. **Investing in the skill development of teachers** (up-gradation and refresher courses, app-based interventions)

 HDFC Bank Ltd, in collaboration with ZIIEI (Zero Investment Innovation for Education Initiative), aspires to change the education system in the country through the 'Teaching The Teacher'. This novel program was designed to improve over 15 lakh teachers' teaching skills across twenty-one states/ union territories, potentially benefiting more than 1.6 crore students.

VII. **Capacity building for the school administration** (school management training, assessment software, etc., that improves school-level administration)

 Wipro's initiative Applying Thought in Schools, focuses on long-term societal development through school education reform and has supported civil society capability development, published quality educational support material, and influenced ideas in education through public advocacy.

VIII. **Setting up specialized educational infrastructure** (establishing technical training institutes, polytechnics, etc.)

 BPCL CSR set up Skill Development Institutes (SDIs) to educate and empower the youth and marginalized towards creating an Atmanirbhar Bharat. The SDI in Kochi offers courses in line with the National Skills Qualification Framework (NSQF) and is affiliated with various Sector Skill Councils and NSDC. As a result, 300 youth have already been trained in various technical courses, and a second campus has been planned in Kerala to prepare over 1,000 students every year.

What causes such differences in long-term impact? How can we proactively factor in impact while choosing alternative social investment strategies? These questions require understanding the social impact and its antecedents, the project objectives and nature of the investment made.

When should social impact be assessed?

'Impact assessment is essential and needs to be a continuum, not just a survey at the completion of activities. You can only know the impact if you can compare the before and after of an initiative with specific metrics.'

—Ramraj Pai, President, Crisil Foundation.

Before the beginning of the project

Projects likely to affect communities usually begin with a baseline assessment through community engagement to understand the social risks and incorporate measures for mitigating the risks and, for example, finding out the level of financial literacy before beginning a financial inclusion project.

On completion of the project

Piramal Foundation, investing majorly in education in over 1,200 government schools in Rajasthan, Gujarat, and Maharashtra, conducts a detailed evaluation of students to measure how much they have learned.

Assessment halfway through a project

ITC Ltd uses impact assessment studies for all its CSR initiatives. Such appraisals have helped the company take stock of projects being implemented on the ground and tweak them.

Assessing lasting impact

Sarojini Damodaran Foundation commissioned a Social Impact Assessment of its Vidhyadhan Scholarship Program. The assessment was undertaken ten years after its commencement to assess how scholarships had helped beneficiaries pursue higher education, get employed, financially and socially uplift their families and contribute to their community.

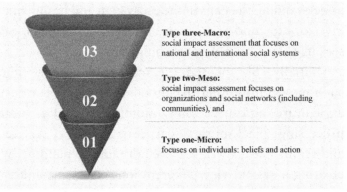

Type three-Macro:
social impact assessment that focuses on
national and international social systems

Type two-Meso:
social impact assessment focuses on
organizations and social networks (including
communities), and

Type one-Micro:
focuses on individuals: beliefs and action

Figure 2: Typology of social impact assessment, Henk A. Becker (2001)

Any discussion on SIA would be incomplete without a holistic view of the business ecosystem. The ecosystem holds

Measuring Breadth and Depth of Social Impact: Selco Foundation

within its fold subparts such as impact investors, technological innovations in new products, and social enterprises trying out different business models designed for underserved markets.

A case in point would be the Selco Foundation (SF), which has incubated social enterprises since 2010. SF believes that social change cannot happen instantaneously as it takes time to change behaviors, engage long-term partners, develop indigenous technologies, and create enduring market linkages. Further, such a sustainable change requires understanding the gaps in the ecosystem and mobilizing investors to fund ecosystem builders/stakeholders. SF sees its role as an ecosystem builder.

Initially, SF focused on sustainable energy but soon moved into other livelihood options like textiles, agriculture, agro-processing, animal husbandry, food processing, blacksmithry, carpentry, pottery, service, and retail. The growth has been organic, expanding by creating a system view wherein long-term sustainable solutions will help the poor withstand a crisis and not slip back into poverty by losing all they had built until then.

What are the pillars of the ecosystem that SF has been building, and how do they ensure sustainable livelihoods?

Financing Solutions
- Financing based on perceived cash flow
- Partnerships with local financial institutions
- Affordable cost of capital
- Appropriate repayment mechanisms
- Appropriate ownership models (individual, operator, rental, community owned)

Policy
- Awareness of informal/micro and small enterprise financial schemes
- Sustainable energy recognition in cross-sector specific schemes (agri, artisan/ craftsmen, manufacturing etc)
- De-risking tools to unlock financing

User & Livelihood Needs

Technology Innovation
- Access to efficient technologies which will build long-term assets/ investments
- Technologies which cater to the actual need and capacity/ market of the entrepreneur/cooperative
- Last-mile supply chains and after sales service

Training & Capacity Building
- Awareness on alternatives to sustain/ improve efficiency in existing vulnerable businesses
- Training to begin new sustainable businesses
- Knowledge transfer on best/worst practices

Channels/ Linkages
- Access to stable input sources (backward linkages)
- Access to consistent or existing or newer linkages to sell end products

Figure 3: Ecosystem Pillars and Gaps

(*Sustainable Energy and Livelihoods: A collection of 50 livelihood applications*)

SF has built an enabling environment with five pillars—financing solutions, technological innovations, training, capacity building, channel linkages, and policy-level changes as the framework for their sustainable livelihoods initiative. Acting as a facilitator, the Foundation undertook pilot projects to demonstrate how the different pillars of the ecosystem need to come together for survival and scaling up, with or without government support. As a result, SF has worked with over 1,500 micro-entrepreneurs, out of whom over 1,000 have improved access to sustainable energy-driven livelihood solutions. Several entrepreneurs expanded their businesses when energy became available for them and their customers. For example, still predominantly labor-intensive, the textile industry is one of the country's largest employment providers. However, small and marginal weavers are on the verge of extinction with the onslaught of large-scale mills and power-driven machinery. The Foundation identified the urgent need for innovative technology to help set up powered machinery with renewable energy for the small weavers, saving their unique skills and exquisite products.

For example, a small-time tailor helped consolidate his business by setting up a solar-powered sewing machine that helped him complete large orders for weddings and festivals. SF helped him get a loan to set up the solar-powered unit, and in six months, he could begin repayment of the loan in monthly installments. A year later, he took another loan to expand his tailoring unit by constructing a bigger room and adding a second solar-powered sewing machine. Timely financing and technological intervention in solar-powered sewing machines enabled him to build a sustainable livelihood; with his first employee joining him on the second machine, prosperity and progress expanded beyond the confines of his home. With a growing business, the tailor is now an employer and a customer with greater purchasing power, giving back to the ecosystem that supports him.

SF's philosophy has always focused on the impact of their interventions on the ecosystem and not just on an individual end-user. Therefore, they recommend assessing impact at three levels: End-user-Enterprise-Ecosystem, bringing in depth and breadth in impact assessment as depicted below.

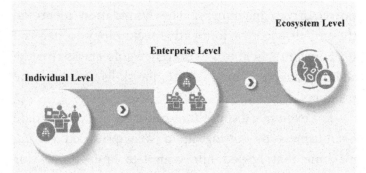

Figure 4: Selco Foundation: Triple-Level Impact Assessment

How to assess impact?

If you were required to undertake an SIA, where should you start? Begin with collecting data—SIA involves collecting information on the number of project beneficiaries or families impacted by the development project. This information includes their detailed socio-economic profile, such as their religion, occupation, family income, and age, and the available education and health facilities.

The collected information can be used for several purposes, depending on the objective of the assessment. For example, suppose it is a proactive assessment to avert possible negative consequences of a project (like setting up a new cement factory or nuclear power plant). In that case, the information will be collected at three stages: pre-construction, during construction, and after completion of the project. This information forms the base for drawing out a resettlement and rehabilitation plan. On the other hand, suppose it is a post-facto assessment of a project. Then, data collection must be after a reasonable time to assess developmental outcomes like improved learning, completion of higher education, increased employment opportunities, higher income/wages, improved standard of living, etc. The time taken from data collection to the preparation of the impact report will depend on the project's size and the initial objectives the project set out to achieve.

Let us illustrate the process of SIA using an example.

Multidimensional, multi-level impact assessment: An example of the Vidhyadhan Scholarship Program

> *Making the dream of higher education a reality and transforming the lives of multiple generations.*

Despite the government's continued efforts over several decades, India continues to be a place where inequalities persist. The prevalence of inequity is particularly problematic concerning access to higher education. The lack of education and consequent inability to land better jobs continue to keep individuals and families wedged in a vicious cycle of poverty.

The problem

Economic deprivation brings in its wake several other deprivations. For instance, most colleges of higher education are located in towns and cities. Social marginalization and lack of information keep the poor from knowing how and when to apply. Students from socio-economically weaker sections often lack the resources to travel to towns for interviews and admissions. Finally, if enrolled, they are unable to bear the substantial burden of boarding and lodging expenses throughout the study's duration.

The program

To help alleviate these disparities and inequities, SDF Foundation offered scholarships to students from economically disadvantaged backgrounds in 1995 in Kerala and other South Indian states. The state government* provides free schooling (without fees or expenses on uniforms, textbooks, midday meals, and transportation) for all children aged 6–14. Still, it has few provisions to make college education (that builds skills and professional capabilities) affordable. The scholarship was offered to academically bright children, primarily from Below Poverty Line (BPL) families, who completed high school (class 10 in India) for higher education scholarships after a rigorous selection process that included tests, interviews, and house visits. Since its inception, the program has provided 13,500 scholarships, with over 10,000 beneficiaries pursuing their higher studies across ten states.

The program was an exciting project from an impact assessment standpoint. The efficacy of a scholarship program comes from its ability to enable education and the consequent developments it can bring about. Further, many developmental benefits can be realized only when better education cascades into the immediate family's betterment and subsequently

---

* Government of Kerala, https://kerala.gov.in/.

over to the community. The indicators of impact, therefore, had to capture this ripple effect adequately.

Framework for assessment

We developed a set of impact indicators based on the Human Capital Approach and Human Capabilities Approach. The impact indicators were assessed by the beneficiaries and their families and community members. This multi-level assessment has the advantage of identifying the ripple effect of a scholarship beyond the individual benefit to the socio-economic improvement for their family members and the broader community.

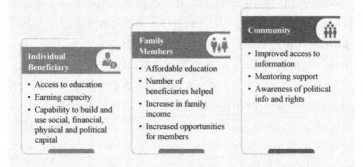

Figure 5: Levels of Beneficiaries Chosen to Assess the Impact

Education can kick-start a capability-building process that enables individuals to generate various forms of capital, viz. human capital (i.e., knowledge and skills), social capital (i.e., respect from others, social and professional networks), political capital (i.e., awareness of rights, opportunities, and sources of support). Subsequently, employment enables them to build financial capital (i.e., savings, investments, insurance, pension, etc.) and physical resources (i.e., amenities, houses, land, etc.). It is assumed that individuals will then be able to use this capital to overcome the perils of poverty, including economic deprivation and exclusion from opportunities, thereby contributing to their empowerment and ability to transform their lives, families, and communities. Therefore, we assessed the multiple dimensions of capital generated and used to escape poverty and improve living standards.

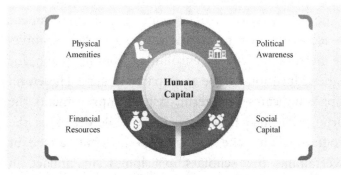

Figure 6: Multiple Dimensions of Resources for Assessment

Objectives, outcomes, and impact

The starting point of meaningful and value-adding interventions is setting a CSR vision for the organization. A clear vision can be a beacon, guiding the interventions' design with intended long-term changes. Unfortunately, the absence of the same often leads to ad hoc giving that fails to convey a coherent message about the social responsibility approach.

The process of implementing the intervention—either internally through the CSR department as an implementation partner, a foundation or an NGO—is crucial in ensuring the successful translation of objectives into perceptible outcomes. Outcomes are the changes that can be ascertained at the end of the project. They are usually immediate improvements like a better understanding of a subject by students taught in a corporate education intervention. On the other hand, impact measures the broader changes brought about in the beneficiaries' lives, community, or environment on account of the intervention. In our earlier example, the increase in students' enrollment from the school for higher education will be an impact measure. Therefore, impact indicates long-term, lasting improvements the corporation may have envisioned while designing the program. Thus, the Vidhyadhan program aimed at ascertaining the scholarship's long-term impact in improving beneficiaries' employment prospects and elevating their family and community to a better life.

Process of assessment

We developed detailed questionnaires to elicit information on developments in human capital, knowledge and capabilities of the beneficiaries, their access to social networks and people of influence, their knowledge of, and their ability to exercise their political capital. We also collected data on financial resources they could garner through employment and, finally, the physical capital they could build for themselves and their families. Questionnaires were separately developed for all three categories of respondents. Data on human, social, and political capital was collected from all beneficiaries, whereas data on financial and physical means were collected from those employed. Attitudinal scales measured human, social, and political capital generation and use. Actual data was sought concerning financial and physical resources regarding the financial provisions made and physical assets purchased.

From outcomes to impact

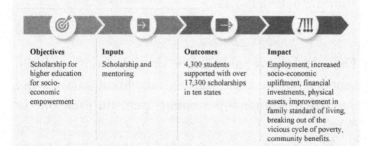

Objectives	Inputs	Outcomes	Impact
Scholarship for higher education for socio-economic empowerment	Scholarship and mentoring	4,300 students supported with over 17,300 scholarships in ten states	Employment, increased socio-economic upliftment, financial investments, physical assets, improvement in family standard of living, breaking out of the vicious cycle of poverty, community benefits.

Results of the impact assessment revealed that the scholarship was very effective in improving course completion rates. It also increased net earnings to approximately thrice as much of the scholarship amount in the first year of employment, with almost 100 percent of the employed beneficiaries able to take their families above the poverty line within a couple of years of work. The overall average return rate indicates that the net earnings (i.e., earnings minus scholarship investment) in the first year of employment were close to twice as much of the total scholarship amount. It was calculated, as shown below:

Rate of Return (RoR)

Rates of return on the scholarship investment per beneficiary in the first year of employment indicate the percentage earning over and above the scholarship amount invested.

They are calculated as $$\frac{(\text{Starting Salary-Scholarship Investment per beneficiary}) \times 100}{\text{Scholarship Investment per Beneficiary}}$$

The calculations are based on the data from employed beneficiaries on their starting take-home salaries and the actual scholarship amount spent on each one of them.

Multipliers, i.e., projected earnings of future beneficiaries in the first year of employment, were calculated as a ratio of starting salary and the scholarship investment, i.e., $\dfrac{\text{Starting Salary}}{\text{Total Scholarship Investment per Beneficiary}}$

Evidence indicates that almost 100 percent of the employed beneficiaries could take their families above the poverty line within a couple of years of employment, an applaudable outcome. Beneficiaries could bag annual salaries thrice the scholarship amounts in the first year of employment. There were concurrent developments reported in their social capital, generation of increased awareness of opportunities, rights, and institutional support sources for the beneficiaries and their family and community, thereby indicating a ripple effect. Earnings helped fund household expenses, siblings' education, and the purchase of amenities that improved lifestyle. The wider community was supported through small loans and educational funding. As assessed for this program, social impact provided a holistic picture of the growth of the student beneficiary and the ripple effect on the family and community.

Part 3

Pathway 2—Social and Sustainable Business Innovation

'We can supplement the government's initiatives by providing a modern platform for sustainable agricultural services and promote consumption in a shared economy. The primary objective is to create a larger value through a product and services model.'
—S. Sivakumar, Group Head Agri & IT, ITC

5

Corporate Social Innovation: Widening the Scope of Corporate Innovation

Kiran was on the way from Delhi to Ghaziabad for a distributors' meet. The food products company where she held a mid-managerial position had launched a new range of snacks. Kiran was determined to use the opportunity to grab greater market share from their competitor, who was leading in western Uttar Pradesh, a territory that was recently added to her portfolio. If she could do that, a promotion that she was eyeing would be hers. Kiran dreamily gazed at the silhouette of a distant hill shrouded in the mist along the highway.

As the car got closer, the birds circling the hill and the trucks trudging along the winding roads to the top became visible. Soon, she felt a stench and realized that it was no dreamy hill but a massive landfill. She had never seen anything like *it. 'My goodness!' a gasp escaped her. The driver smiled, 'First time seeing it, madam? This is the famous Ghazipur landfill. It is as tall as Qutab Minar, someone told me. It will beat the Taj Mahal soon. Quite a national monument, hain nah?'** *Kiran shook her head in disbelief. 'People should be really mindful of the waste they generate, and the government should come up with better waste management facilities,' she said animatedly.*

The driver smiled again, 'What will people do, madam? Everything we buy comes in so much plastic, even potato chips and snacks. Some jholawallahs (NGO members) who came to my daughter's school said it takes eighty years for a potato chips bag to decompose.† But if we do not buy it, you will lose your job, hain nah?' Seeing Kiran's face redden in the rearview mirror, the driver felt he had overstepped his boundaries. 'Sorry, madam, I spoke a little too much,' he said quickly. 'It is okay. What you said is right,' Kiran managed to mutter.

~

---

* Mayank Aggarwal, 'India's megacities, Mumbai and Delhi, sitting on a pile of waste', Mongabay, 11 October 2019, https://india. mongabay.com/2019/10/indias-megacities-mumbai-and-delhi-sitting-on-a-pile-of-waste/.

† Emily Prince, 'Buried crisp packet from 20 years ago, sheds light on rate everyday items decompose', *Eastern Daily Press*, 22 April 2019, https://www.edp24.co.uk/news/crisp-packet-from-20-years-ago-shows-rate-everyday-items-1384380.

The bottom line drives the corporate world. The aim is to register more profit than the previous year and surpass the previous year's growth rates. The performance goals for managers reflect this. Individual performance targets cascading down from the corporate targets ensure that managers' pay and career growth are tied to the bottom line. With such an approach, managers are expected to behave like racehorses with blinders on, trained to look at nothing else other than the goal in front of them. They race forward, faster and faster, generating revenue for the shareholders who have betted on them. That is what matters, or so we are conditioned to think.

Management education in India is a post-Independence phenomenon. Our first publicly funded schools of business—IIM Ahmedabad and IIM Calcutta—were established after India gained independence. The aim was to train managers who could help build the industrial base for a young nation. But, as in business schools worldwide established in the post-war period, India's management education was also based on imported American models rooted in capitalistic ideals.* As India remained a controlled economy, capitalist-style chasing profits could not flourish for an extended period.

Nevertheless, with the liberalization in the 1990s, more unrestrained expressions and pursuance of capitalist ambitions became more prevalent, fueling the

---

* R. Westwood and G. Jack, 'The US commercial-military-political complex and the emergence of international business and management studies', *Critical Perspectives on International Business*, 4(4), (2008): 367–88.

growth of the private sector corporates. The changes in economic policies were meant to facilitate this. Interestingly, this was coupled with a nationalistic spirit, showing the world that India was capable of. The corporate sector looks for 'go-getters' who can help them realize their profit and growth goals. This, in turn, has shaped the self-perceptions and career aspirations of the young MBAs—they see themselves as 'achievers' and would like to be on fast-track career paths of reputed corporates, climbing ladders as quickly as they can. As an ex-CEO of a big consulting firm put it, the young managers transform into 'corporate mercenaries' on a mission with a singular focus on profits. All their talent, creativity, and innovation feed the bottom line.

However, the question facing us now is—can we afford to continue in the same mode? When the pile of garbage we have created while chasing profits is heaping up every single day, can our focus remain exclusively on profits? Will our business models be sustainable, even from a profit-generation perspective? Will we be spared from the crises resulting from the neglect of the societies and environment in which we do business? The Covid-19 pandemic showed us that it will likely reach a state and scale where none of us can escape. Many ultra-rich left India for other countries during the pandemic in chartered private jets,* but if

---

* 'Rich Indians flee by private jet as Covid-19 infections spiral', *Hindustan Times*, 26 April 2021, https://www.hindustantimes.com/india-news/rich-indians-flee-by-private-jet-as-covid-19-infections-spiral-101619448267544.html.

we precipitate crises that affect the entire globe, there is no other planet to escape to (at least not so far). Or should we run our businesses a little differently?

Bottom line to triple bottom line

The above concerns are not new. Academics, business leaders, and policymakers have debated them for decades, generating a whole range of ideas for broadening the purpose of businesses. An important and perhaps the most widely known one is Triple Bottom Line (known as TBL, 3BL, or 3Ps). John Elkington introduced the term Triple Bottom Line in 1994 to challenge business leaders to rethink their purpose.* The idea was to replace the notion of the bottom line, which focused singularly on 'profits', with an expanded version that included 'people' and 'planet'. This was an invitation for corporate leaders to radically overhaul their business models by paying equal attention to all 3 Ps—profit, people, and the planet. The Triple Bottom Line approach requires businesses to track and manage the economic, social, and environmental value-added or destroyed.†

---

* John Elkington, '25 Years Ago I Coined the Phrase "Triple Bottom Line." Here's Why It's Time to Rethink It', *Harvard Business Review*, 25 June 2018, https://hbr.org/2018/06/25-years-ago-i-coined-the-phrase-triple-bottom-line-heres-why-im-giving-up-on-it.
† Jeroen Kraaijenbrink, 'What The 3Ps Of The Triple Bottom Line Really Mean', *Forbes*, 10 December 2019, https://www.forbes.com/sites/jeroenkraaijenbrink/2019/12/10/what-the-3ps-of-the-triple-bottom-line-really-mean/?sh=40d592305143.

- *People:* The positive and negative impact the corporate has on all its key stakeholders, including employees and their families, customers, suppliers, channel partners, community, and any other group that influences or is affected by the business.
- *Planet:* The positive as well as negative impact the corporate has on the natural environment. This includes removing, reducing, or managing waste, reforestation, and other restorative activities to repair the harm caused to nature, reducing the carbon footprint, and judicious use of natural resources and toxic materials.
- *Profit:* The positive and negative impact the corporate has on the local, national, and international economy. Notably, profits here include more than the profit accrued to the corporate, encompassing employment generation, tax contributions, wealth creation, and innovations.

The idea of Triple Bottom Line has inspired the introduction of platforms such as the Global Reporting Initiative (GRI) and Dow Jones Sustainability Indexes (DJSI), which enable comparison of corporate performance on all 3 Ps rather than profit alone. It has also generated a range of corporate accounting and reporting frameworks and standards to bring greater transparency and uniformity in assessing performance on the 3 Ps. These include Social Return on Investment (SROI), ESG (a financial analysis framework considering the Environmental, Social, and Governance factors), and the Trucost approach. However, rather than becoming a reporting paradigm, Elkington hoped that Triple Bottom Line would prompt fundamental shifts in stakeholder engagement and corporate strategy.

Enter Corporate Social Innovation (CSI)

The above is an invitation to organizations to expand the scope of corporate innovation and transform it into Corporate Social Innovation (CSI). Social innovations are novel solutions to social and environmental problem that are more effective, efficient, or just than existing solutions. The value created accrues primarily to society rather than private individuals or organizations.* Corporations are highly innovative in creating business plans and technologies to help them generate greater profits. By daring the corporates to expand their focus to people and the planet, CSI would enable steering the corporate creativity and innovations to address pressing social and environmental issues.

Bringing people-focus to corporate innovation

In the corporate world, usually, the people that matter are the shareholders. It is taken for granted

---

* J. Phills et al., 'Rediscovering social innovation', *Stanford Social Innovation Review*, 6(4), (2008): 34–43.

that the interests of the shareholders come first, and the interests of other stakeholders are only secondary or lower in the hierarchy of importance. Maximising Shareholder Value (MSV), the foundational principle of shareholder capitalism, is the tenet by which the corporate world functions.

Interestingly, this undue prominence of shareholders was not part and parcel of capitalistic ideals until the late 1960s. The shared perspective from the 1930s was that the corporates should cater to the interests of all stakeholders.* That was the argument favoring shifting management responsibilities from the owners to professional managers. It was believed professional managers would be more neutral and therefore strive to serve all stakeholders equally. However, the discourse changed with Milton Friedman's article in the *New York Times* in 1970. Friedman argued that attending equally to all stakeholder interests is impossible in reality, and attempts to strike a balance among all conflicting interests would allow the professional managers to perform only sub-optimally. They would have to assign priorities among the varied stakeholder groups in a practical scenario, and without an explicit hierarchy among stakeholders, the professional managers might prioritize as they please. Friedman

---

* Steve Denning, 'Why Stakeholder Capitalism Will Fail', *Forbes*, 5 January 2020, https://www.forbes.com/sites/stevedenning/2020/01/05/why-stakeholder-capitalism-will-fail/?sh=3dd958f7785a.

argued that shareholders, as owners, were the ultimate risk-takers, as they were entitled only to the residual profits of the organization subsequent to all other stakeholder claims had been satisfied and therefore deserved to be prioritized among all the stakeholders. He proposed that the singular focus on the one goal of maximizing the value for shareholders would enable professional managers to perform optimally rather than trying to satisfy all. The idea—now named 'shareholder capitalism'—caught on and seems to be the maxim corporates believe in and operate on.

Nearly four decades later, having recognized that the above approach has not been exactly good for societal well-being (Remember the 2008 sub-prime lending crisis in the US and subsequent global economic meltdown), the debate is back on who are the people that should matter to corporates.* After the 2008 global financial crisis, shareholder capitalism went down in popularity in academic and corporate circles. Harvard professors Joseph Bower and Lynn Paine pointed out that the practice of shareholder capitalism was 'damaging'. At the same time, the corporate veteran Jack Welch denounced it all together as the 'dumbest idea'. This has led to the re-entry of 'stakeholder capitalism', which recognizes employees, customers, suppliers, and the community as equal shareholders.

---

* Doug Sundheim and Kate Starr, 'Making Stakeholder Capitalism a Reality', *Harvard Business Review*, 22 January 2020, https://hbr. org/2020/01/making-stakeholder-capitalism-a-reality.

Stakeholder capitalism made its way into the Business Roundtable 2019 and was endorsed by 200 CEOs of large corporations.* It has found an avid champion in Klaus Schwab, Founder and Executive Chairman of the World Economic Forum, who advanced it as the central theme of Davos Manifesto 2020.

With influential proponents such as the above in the academic, policy, and practice circles, 'stakeholder capitalism' is here to stay. There is mounting pressure on corporates to take more visible and measurable actions to support all stakeholders. While it does not discard corporate valuation based on value generated for the shareholders, corporates will soon be ranked based on additional parameters capturing value created for the rest of the stakeholders. The advocates of stakeholder capitalism make earnest appeals to the corporates to relook at their existing business models and find ways to be more inclusive of and responsive to stakeholder groups undermined thus far. This has led to a flurry of innovations for corporates worldwide.

Indian corporates are slowly beginning to catch up with this global trend. Unlike the early years of liberalization, when the talk was more centered on market shares, profits, and growth rates, the discussion is being steered to the well-being of the stakeholders.

---

* Steve Denning, 'Why Maximizing Shareholder Value Is Finally Dying', *Forbes*, 19 August 2019, https://www.forbes.com/sites/stevedenning/2019/08/19/why-maximizing-shareholder-value-is-finally-dying/?sh=4f0a7ebe6746.

The impact that they have on people's lives is attracting greater prominence. Corporates are now more willing to experiment with innovations likely to benefit marginalized stakeholders, even if the returns might be low. They aim to understand each stakeholder group's specific circumstances and challenges and devise innovative means for creating value for them. For example, recognizing the difficulties women small business owners face in accessing markets for their products, Amazon India launched the Amazon Saheli program.

Similarly, ITC created e-Choupal to provide information and advisory services to the farmers at the bottom of their supply chain (See the boxes for the cases). Such initiatives differ from the CSR initiatives rooted in a philanthropic approach, where corporations get no financial benefit. These are more tied to the main business of the corporates, as can be seen in Amazon Saheli and ITC e-Choupal cases. While the corporates derive financial benefits from such innovations, such benefits do not accrue exclusively to the corporates. For instance, in the case of ITC e-Choupal, ITC enjoys a steady supply of quality products from the farmers using the service, but the farmers are free to sell their produce to other buyers.

A friend to help women entrepreneurs grow their business far and wide: Amazon Saheli Program

Entrepreneurship is often the only option for the poor to escape poverty. Women have been part of several government empowerment initiatives that advocate entrepreneurship to use their skills to develop a small enterprise that can grow into the primary source of income for the family. Nevertheless, gaining access to markets is one of the challenges in growing into a sustainable enterprise.

Amazon, the world's largest e-commerce company, has started an initiative to help women by giving them space in the most sought-after shopfront to showcase their products. The Saheli Store on its platform is a dedicated store wherein women entrepreneurs from different parts of the country can reach their local produce products online to the most extensive customer base. Many products like handicrafts, apparel, handbags, home décor items, toiletries, herbal hair oils, and cosmetics have a uniquely local flavor and have gone pan India through Amazon.

Saheli (meaning a friend), as the initiative has been aptly christened, helps women entrepreneurs sell on Amazon, benefiting from subsidized referral fees. Once accepted into the program, the entrepreneur gets training to capture images, catalog their products, and develop online product descriptions. Free onboarding, training, and continued mentoring have created several success stories of women entrepreneurs benefiting from the fast-growing digital economy. The women are benefitted from world-class logistics and fulfillment facilities and support and mentoring in account management. In addition, specialized storefronts enable differentiation of products, and the various promotions help the women gain more visibility and thereby grow a loyal customer base.

The Saheli program has many partners committed to women's empowerment in bringing more women under the program's umbrella. Some partner organizations include Kudumbashree, Anubhuti, America Indian Foundation, Mann Desi Foundation, GreenBug, Impulse, and Rangasutra, to name a few.

Source: https://yourstory.com/2017/11/amazon-launches-saheli-programme-to-empower-women-entrepreneurs-in-india

ITC e-Choupal: Revolutionizing agri-business through technology innovation

Indian agri-business had been globally uncompetitive due to the low productivity of its fragmented farms, weak infrastructure, and numerous intermediaries who eat into the farmer's earnings. In June 2000, ITC launched e-Choupal, one of rural India's most extensive Internet-based interventions. By setting up an efficient supply chain to deliver value to its customers, the initiative has enhanced earnings and transformed the livelihoods of over 4 million farmers in over 35,000 villages through 6100 kiosks across ten states in India.

e-Choupal deploys information technology to virtually cluster all the value chain participants and vertically integrate various agricultural supply chain actors. Village internet kiosks set up to access information are managed by farmers who get information on the weather and market prices in their mother tongue. The kiosks also provide information on scientific farm practices and risk management. Farmers can use the kiosks to purchase farm inputs and get them to their doorstep. Real-time information has enabled farmers to make better decisions aligned with market demand. e-Choupal has eliminated wasteful intermediaries and significantly reduced transaction costs. The farmers have benefited through improved farm productivity and higher prices for their produce, triggering a virtuous cycle of increased earnings, enlarged capacity for risk, more significant investments, and a further improvement in quality and productivity. Growth in rural incomes has unleashed the latent demand for industrial goods, propelling the economy into a higher growth trajectory.

ITC's e-Choupal has won numerous awards, including the United Nations Industrial Development Organization (UNIDO) Award at the international conference on Sharing Innovative Agribusiness Solutions 2008 at Cairo, The Ashoka-Changemakers 'Health for All' Award 2006 for the Rural Health Services model for delivery of health services through the e-Choupals and the Stockholm Challenge 2006 award for using information technology for the economic development of rural communities.

Source: https://www.itcportal.com/businesses/agri-business/e-choupal.aspx

Bringing a planet-focus to corporate innovation

Corporations traditionally looked at our environment as a source of resources for production and followed a linear model of 'take-make-waste' in using those resources. There have been warnings for decades about the dangers of such a mindset. However, most corporates have begun to take them seriously only recently as the drastic effects of climate change have become unignorable. It is evident that our approach to the environment has to change, and various ideas are under discussion.

One of the more recent and comprehensive ideas is that of a circular economy.* A circular economy refers to an economy that is regenerative and restorative by design. It aims to replace the prevalent linear model with a circular approach to the use of resources. It stems from the recognition that our resources are finite and puts forward the premise that growth does not have to depend on using limited resources. Instead, the modes of production should focus on eliminating waste and ensuring the continual use of resources. Circular production systems incorporate reuse, repair, refurbishment, remanufacturing, and recycling in the production process to reduce the need for new resources and waste creation.

International agencies and consortiums have come together to promote adopting a circular economy approach among corporates. A key one is Platform for Accelerating the Circular Economy (PACE), jointly launched by the World Economic Forum, Philips, Ellen MacArthur Foundation, United Nations Environment

---

* 'The circular economy in detail', Ellen MacArthur Foundation, https://www.ellenmacarthurfoundation.org/explore/the-circular-economy-in-detail.

Programme, and 40+ other partners in 2018.*
Agencies that develop standards are already on the
task of designing circular economy standards. British
Standards Institution (BSI) launched the BS 8001:2017
Framework for organizational-level implementation of
circular economy principles in 2017. The International
Organization for Standardization (ISO) is developing
four new standards.

With the availability of such knowledge resources,
the backing of influential agencies, and pressure from
the public, the time is ripe for the corporate sector
to pioneer innovations that are better for the planet.
The Ellen MacArthur Foundation suggests three
foundational principles.

- *Design out waste and pollution:* Create your
  designs to use only as few resources as possible
  and generate only a minimal amount of waste and
  pollutants.
- *Keep products and materials in use*: To build a
  production system that 'uses' things rather than 'uses
  them up'. Consider reuse, repair, refurbishment,
  and recycling possibilities in manufacturing. In
  pricing models, consider 'sharing' models rather
  than 'ownership' models.
- *Regenerate natural systems*: Avoid using non-
  renewable resources and rely on renewable ones—

* Platform for Accelerating the Circular Economy, https://
pacecircular.org/.

incorporate processes for replenishing the natural resources in the production system and business models.

According to Ellen MacArthur Foundation, with a young population and emerging manufacturing sector, India is well-positioned to switch to a circular economy. They predict this will set India on a path of 'positive, regenerative and value-creating development'. Such a development could help India generate an annual value of Rs 40 lakh crore (US$ 624 billion), amounting to 30 percent of the current GDP and a 44 percent reduction in greenhouse gas emissions by 2050. Innovations based on circular economy principles will likely impact the construction and real estate, food and agriculture, and automobile industries.*

Indian corporates are becoming more conscious of the environmental impact of their businesses. They are beginning to include environment-related targets among the corporate goals. These include reducing carbon footprint, using renewable energy sources, reducing plastic and other waste, regenerating soil and water sources, etc. They actively track their progress and share it with the broader stakeholders. For instance, several FMCG and retailing companies have begun thinking deeply about tackling plastic waste (See the case in the box).

---

* 'Circular economy in India: Rethinking growth for long-term prosperity', Ellen MacArthur Foundation, https://ellenmacarthurfoundation.org/circular-economy-in-india.

Working towards a circular economy: Plastic waste management by corporates and their stakeholders

Come monsoon season, clogged drains and wastewater overflowing into the roads and sometimes into housing society compounds and schools is common in Indian metros. Mumbai has its annual tryst with flooding almost every year now. Such health hazards are not an act of nature. Instead, they are caused by the clogging of drains by plastics that are carelessly dumped. While the sachet has revolutionized packaging in India, bringing products packaged in small quantities within reach of the bottom of the pyramid consumers, the environmental costs of the lower unit price FMCG products have been very high. Throw-away plastic packaging is choking our drains, polluting rivers, endangering freshwater sources that feed our cities, and finally exposing us to cancers of various kinds.

FMCG companies have finally acknowledged their implicit role in this hazardous reality and have launched several measures to stem the environmental damage and step up their commitment to their stakeholders.

HUL is a leading player in the FMCG space declaring its contribution to building a circular economy that creates no waste by recycling plastics. The company announced that starting in 2021 it will collect and process more plastic packaging waste than the plastic they use in its packaging. It is estimated that over 1 lakh tons of post-consumer plastic waste will be collected through partner agencies across India. In collaboration with Reliance SMART, the company collects plastic waste from customers who can dispose of used plastics at the store recycle bins. Reliance offers a model for retailers to join hands in facilitating plastic waste collection and recycling. Several organizations with skills in collecting, segregating, and recycling plastic waste have joined forces with HUL in the clean-up. Saahas, Carpe, Recykal, Planet Savers, RaddiConnect, Geocycle, and RamkyEnviro are working with municipal corporations to make the plastic waste collection more efficient. Reiterating the need for a joint effort, HUL's chairman and managing director Sanjiv Mehta share his company's mission to work with key stakeholders to ensure that plastic stays in the economy and out of the environment. He believes that waste management is a collective responsibility wherein stakeholders must collaborate to protect the environment from being overrun by plastic waste. Working with stakeholders includes making waste collection and segregation safer for the workers involved in waste collection. HUL has implemented an Extended Producer Responsibility (EPR) framework for plastic waste management, helping develop an ecosystem of partners for safely processing plastic waste.

Others like ITC, Coca-Cola, Dabur India, Flipkart, and Amazon have also set ambitious targets in plastic waste management. ITC, for instance, is working towards exclusively using recyclable and reusable or compostable packaging over the next decade. Dabur India has collected and processed 20 million kilos of plastic waste by March 2021.

Source:https://www.greenqueen.com.hk/plastic-neutral-fmcg-hindustan-unilever-to-achieve-100-plastic-waste-collection-in-2021/

By no means are these easy changes to make. They require a radical rethinking of the existing designs and business models, investment, and deeper-level changes in organizational functioning. However, this does not mean only resource-rich MNCs and large corporates can do this. We have seen MSME sector companies taking innovative approaches to recycling and re-productizing waste material with the help of the latest technologies. For example, Rhino Machines, an MSME company from Anand, Gujarat, uses the waste from its foundry business to make silica blocks. More importantly, they have made their innovation available in the public domain for foundries worldwide to emulate (See the box).

Value from waste: A socially responsible business innovation

The problem of plastic waste has grown in gigantic proportions in the country. The 2018–19 report by the Central Pollution Control Board (CPCB) estimated the annual plastic waste generated and dumped in the country to be 3.3 million metric tonnes yearly. However, given the challenges in collecting precise data about waste generation, there are genuine fears that the actual amount may be higher. Not only does this remind us of the impending apocalypse of being inundated with non-degradable plastic waste, but the problem also is growing as people become more affluent and consume more FMCG products. For instance, states like Goa and Delhi contribute around 60 gm and 37 gm per capita per day, respectively—against a national average of 8 gm per day.* The problem typifies our callous and deteriorating relationship with nature, which will not go away once we shift the waste out of our homes to the municipal dumps far out of sight. Plastic waste has found its way into our rivers, water bodies, our landfills, where it will stay forever and ultimately into our bodies through our food chain.

---

* 'Plastic Waste is India's & World's Most Formidable Environmental Challenge', Realty Plus, 17 October 2020, https://www.rprealtyplus.com/interviews/plastic-waste-is-indias-worlds-most-formidable-environmental-challenge-79284.html.

Socially responsible business innovation is one of the significant ways organizations can co-opt their thinking and resources to solve societal problems—a commendable initiative by Rhino Machines* from Anand, Gujarat. Rhino is a full-fledged manufacturing firm producing conventional green sand, pouring, and centrifugal casting products. International collaborations with global industry leaders like Fondarc (France) and Found Equip (Italy) helped the company evolve into a truly global player providing an exhaustive range of cutting-edge foundry equipment. Rhino stands tall on its twin mission statements: (1) working towards converting Waste to Wealth using plastic waste and dust collected from the foundry to usable bricks and paver blocks and (2) creating job and business opportunities for sustainable living.

Rhino conceptualized this project, wherein silica plastic blocks are manufactured using recycled foundry dust/sand waste (80 percent) and mixed plastic waste (20 percent). R+D design studios collaborated with Rhino in creating the prototype. Several rounds of iterations led to the final product, which is both zero waste and very competitive in the cost of production. Another advantage of the product is that it can be very competitively priced compared to the conventional and commonly available red clay brick.

* Rhino Machines Pvt. Ltd., https://www.rhinomachines.net/index. php/aboutus.

The raw materials were the clean plastic waste from hospitals, societies, individuals, social organizations, and local municipal corporations, including 6 tonnes of plastic waste and 16 tonnes of dust and sand collected for recycling from the foundry industry. What was challenging to dispose of somehow became a material of value in a social value creation process.

Going beyond product innovation, Rhino Machine is now creating an ecosystem solution so that foundries worldwide can manufacture and distribute paver blocks and significantly reduce plastic waste's impact on the environment. The versatile blocks are excellent for building walls, toilets, school campuses, health clinics, pavers, driveways, and more. Manufacturing the blocks can open up several employment opportunities for rural youth. Creating value out of waste could set an example of business innovation that can convert a problem into a socially responsible and environmentally sustainable profitable business venture.

Are we there yet?

The global trend discussed above has inspired several corporates to steer their innovative capacity to address people and planet challenges. This also yields business benefits—the conservative estimate is that UN

Sustainable Development Goals would create market opportunities worth $12 trillion a year by 2030.

However, interestingly, Elkington recalled the concept of Triple Bottom Line in 2018, twenty-five years after it was first introduced. Thus, the Triple Bottom line was intended to be a tool for corporates to make a societal impact by radically changing their fundamental ways of operating. He felt that the concept had been misappropriated by accounting and consulting frameworks and was reduced to a mere reporting tool. Many corporates use it to present themselves as socially impactful when there has been little change in how they conduct business. Although more corporates seemed to endorse social impact ideals, we are still far off from effectively resolving the issues of the people and the planet, Elkington observed.

The critical bottleneck seems to be the last of the 3 Ps: Profit. Corporations tend to define it as the financial profit for themselves narrowly. Elkington's idea of profits was more extensive in scope—it was meant to include the broader economic impact of corporate innovation and action on society at large (and not financial impact alone). Even corporate leaders such as Jack Welsh agree that the narrow focus on shareholder value has to expand to include broader and longer-term value creation. The alternate terminology in OECD Forum in 2015 perhaps offers a new way of understanding the 3Ps: People, Planet and Prosperity.

'Prosperity' seems to better replace 'profits' to convey its intended meaning.

Profit orientation is hard-wired into the corporate psyche. It will be a while before a large majority of the corporate world start looking at 'prosperity' as the legitimate goal for them to pursue rather than 'profits'. Corporations need internal champions to make such a transition possible. If we have more managers committed to changing the older ways of doing things and championing and sustaining socially impactful innovations, we might get there sooner.

6

Championing Corporate Social Innovation: How It Is Done

P.P. Sukumaran (PPS), President-HR of Murugappa Group, left the conference room after a long exhausting meeting. It was a meeting with the top management to review the progress of TQM implementation in their northern Kerala plant. The review was part of the company-wide quality drive rolled out in phases at their various plants. They had substantially streamlined operations in plants where the implementation had reached advanced stages. The agenda of this particular meeting was a related matter—a downsizing decision. They were to let go of 200 workers. PPS (as he was called) had seen it coming from the early days; it was inevitable. Today, it was just a matter of getting the formal nod from the top management.

PPS reached his cabin and sat back in his chair. He found himself brooding. He knew downsizing was something everybody, including the workers perhaps, had expected. He was sure it was a sensible decision for the company. Moreover, they planned to give a generous severance package, so convincing the union might not be too much trouble. However, somehow, he could not take comfort in any of these justifications.

The decision involved 200 families losing their livelihood, he thought to himself. He had often visited the tiny village where the plant was located. It was unlikely that all 200 of them would find alternative employment opportunities there. Knowing the predilections of the menfolk in the region, he was worried that the despair of losing the job and not finding another one would drive them to spend all their severance money on alcohol.

'Oh, what am I to do?' He sighed.*

~

Even in companies serious about CSR—those with generous CSR budgets, which create foundations and promote employee volunteering—social consciousness does not come to the forefront strongly enough for business decisions. This is not surprising. Managers,

---

* L. Poonamallee and S. Joy, 'Connecting the micro to the macro: An exploration of micro-behaviors of individuals who drive CSR initiatives at the macro-level', *Frontiers in Psychology*, 9 (2018): 2417.

trained to make 'good for the business' decisions, are habituated to basing these decisions on profits, growth, market share, and corporate reputation, not essentially 'good for the extent stakeholders'. It is not that they skimp over their contractual or legal obligations to the stakeholders (or environment, for that matter); they may not. However, enacting social consciousness requires going beyond contractual or legal obligations and ensuring the well-being of the people and the planet.

The grand ideas of socially conscious organizations are out there. But how do we make them a reality? It takes people within the organizations to do that. Else, the vision, strategic goals, and targets concerning people and the planet will remain on paper, unactualized. That is where aspiring Impact Champions need to step in.

Steering the organization to a path of social consciousness will require promoting greater introspection and reflection about the current ways of doing things. Leading it to Corporate Social Innovation (CSI) will require radical changes to the existing policies, processes, and practices. This will be an arduous mission as the current ways are deeply ingrained in members of the organization—top to bottom. So why change something, especially if it is fetching good business results? Can't we make amends elsewhere? Is it not enough to collect plastic bags or plant trees and be carbon neutral? Do we have to invent plastic-free packaging or change the production process altogether?

You may have much self-doubt about whether this is a conversation that you can initiate and successfully lead to tangible decisions. 'I do not have a position of power, and I am just starting, you may say. Yes, occupying top positions will make some things easy for sure. Nevertheless, having a top position does not mean that the rest of the organization will buy into what you suggest, just like that. Impact Champions at any level need to undertake long, patient work with the members of their organizations while championing innovative ideas to generate more comprehensive societal benefits. In this chapter, we draw on the research and practice and detail the steps in championing socially innovative business solutions within the corporate context. We do hope that this provides you with both the clarity and confidence that you are looking for.

1. Bring your social consciousness to the office

Do not leave your social consciousness at home when you come to the office. When you operate with a 'corporate mindset' in a regular day's work, you accept and get on with decisions that look perfectly sensible and acceptable from corporate and legal standpoints. However, it takes social consciousness to recognize when stakeholders or environmental interests are being compromised in what looks like business as usual.

In the example we started this chapter with, PPS could have looked at the downsizing decision as part of the job, albeit unfortunate. It was a legitimate and legally compliant business decision. However, he was nonetheless concerned about this decision's potential societal-level negative consequences. It was not that PPS company did not consider workers and families as their stakeholders; they did. However, organizations tend to have narrow conceptualizations of their responsibility to each stakeholder group. They focused on legal responsibilities and worked out good severance packages in this case.

Nevertheless, the more significant societal implications often escape the organizational radar. Impact Champions detect what the organizations miss. PPS was worried about the negative repercussions, even after those workers ceased to be their employees. He wanted to make sure 'that we do not leave behind debris in that sense, we do not leave behind people who may become a social burden'.*

In another example, Seema Prem, CEO of FIA Technology Services, similarly applied her social consciousness. FIA is a Business Correspondence Company intermediary that makes banking services accessible to the poor, remote, rural, and marginalized populations. Business Correspondence companies appoint and manage agents where mainstream

---

* Ibid.

banks refrain from opening branches. The agents provide banking services to the 'unbanked' on behalf of the mainstream banks. The agents and Business Correspondence Companies receive a bank commission for this. While some agents run kiosks, others deliver banking services door-to-door. The Covid-19 outbreak affected many agents' ability to carry on with their operations, which affected their income. As a person deeply committed to gender equality, Seema quickly noticed a disproportionate impact on women's income compared to men. She quickly gathered feedback from the field only to discover that women were under pressure from their families to give up work when lockdowns and related travel restrictions made going to work difficult. This was problematic for her, not only because of the gendered nature of the impact but also because of its larger societal implications. Seema knew women agents served the older, disabled, and marginalized groups of customers more than men did, as those groups found women more approachable. If these women agents were not back in business, the banking services would become inaccessible for the most vulnerable groups yet again.

Thus, the social consciousness of Impact Champions is particularly handy in engendering a more expansive view of the corporate impact on society and the planet. Every organization has multiple stakeholders. The chances are priority is given to stakeholders with relatively more power and legitimacy, whose needs are more urgent and get public attention, and/ or who are more proximate to the decision-makers.* Impact Champions can bring the stakeholders who are rarely prioritized to the forefront and turn corporate attention to the more nuanced aspects of organizational impact in the broader society and planet that might go unnoticed.

2. Appoint yourself as the Impact Champion

Impact Champions take personal responsibility for action. Many who identify issues such as the above refrain from action, even when they feel deep in their heart that they should do something about it. The responses are varied. Some self-justify these as inevitable, though unfortunate, outcomes, and it will be beyond their position and capabilities to fix them. Some point out that there is no incentive for them to do this. These are not part of their role expectations or performance goals. For some, it is someone else's job— maybe the CSR people, the HR, top management, or an external NGO should address such issues.

There will also be another category worried about how they will be perceived if they raise such concerns. Will they be considered troublemakers and woolly-

* R. K. Mitchell et al., 'Toward a theory of stakeholder identification and salience: Defining the principle of who and what counts', *Academy of Management Review*, 22(4), (1997): 853–86.

headed hippies? They would rather conform and not cause a stir. Some half-consider taking action, but the fear of failure stops them. How much ever we wish for it, it is an uphill task. It may not yield outcomes fast, if at all. So why at all try? Another group will park it for later. They feel they might be better prepared to address such concerns later in their career or after leaving the corporate sector.

Nevertheless, a rare few are unperturbed by the above anxieties. For them, the question is: If I don't, who will? If not now, when? Compared to the former categories, which are more extrinsically driven, this latter category is intrinsically driven. They feel that addressing issues that tug at their hearts gives them more job satisfaction and makes life meaningful. They might see this as the legacy of their corporate career rather than money and promotions. It is not that they anticipate success; they do not, in many cases. But they believe it is better to try and fail than not try at all. Their emotional connection with the issue makes them personally invested in satisfactorily solving it.

In the above examples, PPS or Seema's job roles did not require them to address their identified issues. As President-HR, PPS was responsible for the workers only as long as they were in employment; what they did afterward was their own business. But, PPS was determined to do something to ensure their well-being beyond their term of employment. He was not prepared to wash his hands off because there were no formal contractual or compliance obligations or unwritten expectations on the part of the organization or even the affected stakeholders. Instead, he held himself responsible for the action. In the case of Seema, as a CEO of a business that runs on very thin margins, any investment to improve the mobility of the women agents would be a financial burden.

Given that the commissions on services rendered to the most vulnerable groups were among the lowest, such financial investment might not justify the benefits. But Seema also was determined to do something about it. Further, it must be noted that neither of them delegated the job to anyone else, though they were in positions where they could have done that. Championing impact takes personal involvement. Impact Champions do it themselves.

3. Mobilizing partners

You have to do it yourself but cannot do it alone. Irrespective of where you are in the organizational hierarchy, you would need partners. Partners are actors inside (sometimes even outside) the organization committed to addressing societal or environmental problems you seek to solve through organizational means. In addition to moral and emotional support (which you will need aplenty), partners bring legitimacy to the cause (especially if they are higher in the hierarchy or hold formal or informal positions of influence), knowledge, and skills resources to develop a deeper understanding of the issue from multiple perspectives as well as potential solutions, access to networks and organizational resources, and political backing to elicit favorable decisions.

However, winning partners is easier said than done. Everybody would differ in how they see the issue you are trying to raise and how important it is to address it. Here there are 'easy converts' and 'hard converts'. The easy ones you know already think or are likely to feel the same way as you do. So it might take little effort to convince them to get their buy-in.

Nevertheless, the hard converts might interpret the problem entirely differently or consider it a non-issue. Therefore, you need a 'tempered' approach to engage with them.* This means not coming across too strong in your viewpoints but opening up space to reflect on issues and surface their viewpoints. Impact Champions believe that too much conviction about what you say also could be destructive†—it closes up the space for dialogue too soon. The fundamental principle is: do not alienate anyone if you can help it. Convincing the hard converts might take a long time, but as a participant in the research of Wickert and De Bakker (2018)

---

* Debra Meyerson, *Tempered Radicals: How Everyday Leaders Inspire Change at Work*, (Brighton: Harvard Business School Press, 2003).

† C. Wickert and F. G. De Bakker, 'Pitching for social change: Toward a relational approach to selling and buying social issues', *Academy of Management Discoveries*, 4(1), (2018): 50–73.

observed, 'constant dripping of water wears away the stone'.* If you are patient and keep at it, many of them will likely see your point in the end. You might be able to win allies from the opposing camps. In the case of PPS, he reached out to the workers' union and the plant HR. Securing buy-in from both parties, he had them work together to map out the demographic details and skillsets of the families affected by the downsizing decision as to the groundwork for exploring alternative livelihoods for them.

However, getting to action sooner might help form a coalition of early converts to spread awareness, anchor the discussions, and facilitate the generation of solutions. As the coalition takes the conversation to the broader organizational circles, how the issue is 'framed is crucial'. 'Framing' refers to articulating the problem, solution, and why it is vital to address it.† Framing can both attract or alienate the audience. When it comes to the issues of society or the planet, the general tendency is to give it a 'moral framing'—present it as the 'right thing to do'. While some buy it, it has not always been found to elicit requisite support in the corporate world. It is possible to broach the same issue by employing a 'pragmatic' or 'business case framing' and focusing on its benefits. This often gets more supporters. When

---

* Ibid.

† E. Alt and J. B. Craig, 'Selling issues with solutions: Igniting social intrapreneurship in for-profit organizations', *Journal of Management Studies*, 53(5), (2016): 794–820.

Richard Stallman started the Free Software Movement in the 1980s, he framed the proprietary software and licensing practices core to the industry business models as 'morally and ethically wrong' and offered free software development as an alternative. He did not get the industry majors to buy into the movement. However, in 1998, Bruce Perens and Eric Raymond developed the Open Source Software movement. Although it uses the same licensing practices as Free Software, it found supporters among industry majors such as Sun Microsystem. This is attributed to the framing—the Open Source movement stressed practical benefits to the industry rather than moral arguments.*

Although she was moved by the cause of gender parity in Seema's case, that probably was not something that animated her top management, who were all from the mainstream banking and finance industry. Seema arranged for business data to be pulled out to calculate the business potential of investing in mobility solutions for their women agents. This made more sense to the top management, who then got on board.

4. Creating solution prototypes

Raising issues will not solve problems unless you suggest solutions as well. Otherwise, the discussion

---

* G. Von Krogh and E. Von Hippel, 'Special issue on open source software development', *Research Policy*, 32 (2003): 1149–57.

on the issues will create noise and dissipate. Many worthwhile causes have died down that way. For example, soon after the Global Financial Crisis in 2008, there were Occupy Wall Street (OWS) movements in several cities worldwide. Young adults camped out seeking government attention to unfettered capitalism. Although it caught global attention for a while, no real change came out of it, as no recommendation for action could be looked into. Research shows that in the corporate social innovation context, issues raised along with solutions get more significant support and are more likely to progress toward implementation.*

It is not that you must invent new solutions for every issue. Do your homework and explore the solutions that have been tried for similar problems. In all likelihood, you can retool some of them and spare yourself from reinventing the wheel. The benefit is also knowing beforehand what kind of results it has produced in the past and what kind of challenges cropped up in the implementation. That may help you to be better prepared. In the case of PPS, he had actively sought ideas and solutions from his friends in the corporate sector outside of his organization. One of them was Deen, who ran a Business Process Consulting firm. Deen directed PPS to his classmate

---

* P. Bansal, 'From issues to actions: The importance of individual concerns and organizational values in responding to natural environmental issues', *Organization Science*, 14(5), (2003): 510–27.

from graduate school, Dr. Nalini Gangadharan, who was in charge of Livelihood Advancement Business School (LABS), founded by Dr. Reddy's Foundation. LABS had a skilling model that PPS found would be appropriate for retraining their redundant workers to place them in alternative jobs or start their ventures suitably. They involved the workers and their families in the re-skilling program. In addition, local banks were also involved in ensuring that severance packages were prudently saved or invested or used for productive purposes. The program was successful in pre-empting the predicament that PPS was worried about.

If there is no appropriate solution, then do invent your own. These solutions do not have to be grand and comprehensive. The aim is to set the ball rolling and accumulate small wins. In their efforts to help the women agents, Seema and her team at FIA did a diagnostic study. It revealed structural and socio-cultural issues that affected women agents' mobility during the pandemic and their ability to continue working. The critical structural issue was access to their own means of transportation, which most women did not have. As the country locked down, public transport came to a standstill, or people were too scared to use it. Women had to rely on the male members of the family for transportation, who themselves had to go to work and, therefore, were reluctant to ferry women around. The key socio-cultural issue was the families' attitudes to women's employment and income.

In most cases, women were regarded as supplementary income generators for the family. When the pandemic hit, families were prepared to forgo this supplementary income and have women back home for caring responsibilities. Seema and FIA team first chose the structural issue to tackle, as it felt less complex than the socio-cultural one. They considered helping the women agents to get vehicle loans but found that the terms and conditions for vehicle loans were biased against women, and getting a loan took a lot of work. FIA is now trying to raise grant money for funding vehicles for their women agents.

Having a solution, piloting it, and generating early results help get the wider audience's attention and approval. For example, FIA had been trying to impress upon the banks and financial institutions to provide business correspondence services that their customers (all at the Base of the Pyramid) lacked: financial products for wealth management. In particular, they tried to persuade them to create mutual fund products for the BoP, but no heed was paid. Most financial institutions refused to do product innovations for the poor, saying that the transaction costs did not justify the profits. So FIA developed a mutual fund-based product for their BoP customers. Now, having demonstrated the viability of such a product, they anticipate that industry will follow.

5. Institutionalizing the solutions

The solution prototypes and the small wins from piloting them should help you institutionalize your innovation as genuine Corporate Social Innovations. Research shows that rather than grand but abstract organizational vision, the outcomes of which are intangible, smaller pilots with tangible outcomes are more relatable for the audience.* The success of pilots will help generate broader buy-in for the solutions and conviction in their efficacy.

Institutionalizing is not without challenges, however. Compared to the piloting stage, institutionalizing will require more significant resource commitments, and more lasting changes in policies, processes, and practices, creating enabling structures for the organizations. Encouraged by the success of the skilling model in northern Kerala, PPS wanted to bring the model to Chennai, where the company was headquartered. He felt that the model could train the at-risk urban youth and place them in corporate jobs, including within the Murugappa Group. It would help the corporates access better-trained labor while fulfilling their social responsibility to the poor urban communities around them, who could hardly benefit from the opportunities in the liberalized economy. He

---

* C. Wickert and F. G. De Bakker, 'Pitching for social change: Toward a relational approach to selling and buying social issues', *Academy of Management Discoveries*, 4(1), (2018): 50–73.

discussed the idea within his organization and with senior leaders from several Chennai corporations. While all of them recognized it as a great idea, most were hesitant to take part. The key reservation was that it was an approach developed by Dr. Reddy's Foundation, which did not leave a place for them to share credit. So PPS and three friends from other organizations devised an innovative consortium model as the solution. The idea was to create a consortium where several corporates could chip in with funds and share administrative responsibilities. At the same time, Dr. Reddy's Foundation took responsibility for the curriculum, pedagogy, and training delivery. This model permitted sharing ownership and credit, and LABS Chennai was set up as a consortium. This innovative consortium model has since been replicated in other parts of India.

At times, institutionalizing innovations would need more comprehensive ecosystem support. This will require more advocacy work at the industry and policy levels. FIA has been trying to solve the mobility challenges of women agents from their end by securing grants to enable their agents to buy two-wheelers. However, in the process, FIA uncovered the biases in the banks' vehicle loan policies that the banks currently follow, which are detrimental to women. Seema, CEO of FIA, strongly feels that the industry needs to overhaul these policies. She has addressed the issue with policy bodies like NITI Ayog and international agencies like UN Women. She tries to get industry associations and even competitor companies to turn their attention to women's agents' barriers and seek meaningful interventions. To raise awareness and mobilize action, FIA continues to write about the issue in forums such as CGAP.*

Various problems require innovations of multiple complexities. While some issues can be tackled with slight changes in structures, policy, and practice, some might need monumental mental shifts on the part of many actors, and others need advanced science and technology innovations. However, the starting point of all socially-oriented innovations is your social consciousness and willingness to drive innovative change. If you ever feel shaken by the scale of what you have to achieve, take a cue from a climber scaling a peak: You need to focus on where to place your next step. Then, step by step, you will reach there.

---

* 'Freedom on Wheels – A Ride to Economic Empowerment', FinDev Gateway, 9 December 2020, https://www.findevgateway.org/blog/2020/12/freedom-wheels-ride-economic-empowerment.

Part 4

Pathway 3—Social Entrepreneurship

'I'm encouraging young people to become social business entrepreneurs and contribute to the world, rather than just making money. Making money is no fun. Contributing to and changing the world is a lot more fun.'
—Muhummad Yunus, Founder, Grameen Bank

7

Social Entrepreneurship:
Starting Businesses for Social Impact

*According to the WHO World Malaria Report
2017, India had the highest incidents of malaria
outside Sub-Saharan Africa. Even more worrisome
is that our surveillance system was highly inefficient,
and the number of cases was hugely underreported.
The poor are disproportionately affected by the
disease as unsanitary conditions like open drains,
stagnant ponds, and ditches that breed mosquitoes,
the carrier of the vector, are most common in rural
areas and the poorer localities of urban cities. A
study in Lancet (2010) reported that 90 percent
of deaths due to malaria occurred in rural areas,
and 86 percent occurred due to inadequate medical
attention. Our country is committed to combating
the disease with an allocation of Rs 10,653 crore
under the National Strategic Plan for Malaria
Elimination 2017–2022. Any attempt to reduce*

*the death rate must include vector control and,
more importantly, early diagnosis and treatment.
Unfortunately, the number of health workers in the
country trained to use rapid diagnostic test kits to
detect the disease remains woefully inadequate.*

~

Healthcare services in India are regulated by the Union
health ministry and administered by various state
governments. Despite a 69,000-crore budget allocation
to expand health insurance through the Ayushman
Bharat-Pradhan Mantri Jan Aarogya Yojana (PMJAY),
the task of reaching healthcare to the masses is too
humongous for the government to accomplish by itself.
Covering 79 percent of the urbanites and 72 percent of
the rural folks, the private sector has a robust healthcare
presence.* However, they need more incentives to reach
remote locations or offer quality services at the most
affordable prices. Therefore, convincing a corporate
to initiate CSI to solve problems like the above might
be challenging. Furthermore, solutions for such issues
will require more effort and resources than CSR can
afford. If you are an aspiring Impact Champion keen to
address such issues, what can you do?

---

* Siddhartha Bhattacharya, 'Role of private sector towards universal
  health coverage in India', *Times of India*, 6 May 2020, https://
  timesofindia.indiatimes.com/blogs/voices/role-of-private-sector-
  towards-universal-health-coverage-in-india/.

Becoming a social entrepreneur

We are witnessing an increasing number of people in India and the world turn to the entrepreneurial path to find and deploy effective solutions to the persisting social and environmental problems. As social entrepreneurs— entrepreneurs driven by social consciousness and determined to make a social impact, they fill the institutional voids left behind by the public and private sectors. They possess an innate ability to spot unfulfilled requirements in the market and seize the opportunity to replace an inefficient service or unsatisfactory product with valuable solutions for an underserved segment of the market or society. However, while commercial entrepreneurs exploit market opportunities for profit, social entrepreneurs recognize and are enthused by opportunities to create social value.

Most start with a personal vision to change the status quo, but converting that vision into a viable business model requires mission leadership capabilities to assemble and inspire a team to create the organization. A social enterprise is an organizational framework through which social entrepreneurs accomplish their vision. They may also need to build a local ecosystem to support their enterprise. Social entrepreneurs must be particularly adept at establishing relationships with various stakeholders, selling their ideas, spreading awareness, and garnering people to be part of the change.

An example would be Dr. Govindappa Venkataswamy, who started Aravind Eye Hospital, which creates value for all its customers while capturing value only from those who can afford to pay for the services. Dr. V (as he is remembered) set up the first hospital offering top-quality ophthalmological care to the poor at subsidized treatment rates, making a cure for blindness available to all, regardless of their capacity to pay. Initially set up with funds pooled from family members, Dr. V created a business model that treated more than half its patients for free, cross-subsidized by affluent patients. They pay for the most advanced surgical intervention services and facilities like rooms with various comforts. Operational efficiency and lower costs were achieved through economies of scale (with an average of 2,000 surgeries performed annually by a surgeon while the norm at other eye hospitals is around 300).* The intraocular lens's in-house manufacturing is another key feature of its 'high quality, high volume, low cost.'† business model. Efficiency through innovative operative procedures and leadership that empathized with the community are the distinctive elements that the visionary Dr. V ensured at the hospital. The latest ophthalmological

---

* 'Aravind', Business Model Toolbox, https://bmtoolbox.net/stories/aravind/.

† Aravind Krishnan, 'Aravind Eye-Care System – McDonaldization of Eye-Care', Harvard Business School, 9 December 2015, https://digital.hbs.edu/platform-rctom/submission/aravind-eye-care-system-mcdonaldization-of-eye-care/.

surgical interventions helped attract and retain the most qualified doctors, key stakeholders in the business model.

Further, over 60 percent of their workforce comprises local women recruited and trained as technicians who can perform multiple routine tasks. Today, besides the hospital at Madurai, the group has grown to seven tertiary centers, seven secondary centers, six community eye clinics, and eighty vision centers and eye banks. In partnership with local communities, community outreach has ensured awareness and telemedicine access to ophthalmological interventions. This has helped actualize Dr. V's vision of 'reaching the unreachable.'*

Attributes of a Social Entrepreneur

---

* 'Outreach', Aravind Eye Care System, https://aravind.org/outreach/.

Haigh and Hoffman (2012) describe social entrepreneurs as participative leaders with a transformational leadership style. They often strive to bring their values into business, their firms being an avenue to experiment with the change they want to bring about in their environment. Their style exemplifies openness and dialogue, fairness and development orientation, pushing the organization to achieve the highest excellence levels. The enterprise then becomes an authentic expression of how a company should be run, its responsibilities to its stakeholders, and what means are available to do business in a non-exploitative and sustainable fashion. Though propelled by their desire to change, a social entrepreneur must also set up the business and survive in a competitive context, often with little governmental support. Socially conscious consumers have given a fillip to eco-friendly products, and social entrepreneurs have used this opportunity to experiment with alternative and eco-friendly products. One such example is Bare Necessities (See the box).

Bare Necessities: Zero Waste Solutions Pvt Ltd

Though hailing from a family of entrepreneurs, Sahar Mansoor describes herself as an accidental social entrepreneur. Her decision to follow a zero-waste lifestyle that uses no harmful chemicals and is not packaged in plastics led her to a dead end as there were very few such personal care products in the

---

market.* Aghast by the amount of trash generated daily in Indian metros and not wanting to be part of the problem, Sahar launched a range of personal products made from natural ingredients and free of toxic chemicals and eco-friendly recyclable packaging. Her environmental planning, policy, and law background from the University of Cambridge and her work at the World Health Organization and SELCO, a social enterprise, sensitized her to waste management issues and their adverse social consequences. Sahar adopted minimalism as a key to eliminating waste by the continual use of resources, choosing a lifestyle that is 'kinder, humbler and socially driven while still enjoying life's beauties.'† She also realized that consumers must be educated about zero-waste living and conducts brand workshops that propagate mindful consumption. Her social enterprise is managed entirely by women, empowering economically disadvantaged women. Interestingly, women head 24 percent of the over 2 million social enterprises in India, against only 9 percent in mainstream businesses.‡

---

* 'Our Story', Bare Necessities, https://barenecessities.in/pages/our-story.
† Aalika Mahindra, 'The Eternal Optimist', *Verve*, 5 June 2020, https://www.vervemagazine.in/people/the-eternal-optimist-sahar-mansoors-sustainable-zero-waste-lifestyle.
‡ 'The state of social enterprise in Bangladesh, Ghana, India and Pakistan', British Council, 2016, https://www.britishcouncil.org/sites/default/files/bc-report-ch4-india-digital_0.pdf.

What is a social enterprise?

> 'To make life better for many, social entrepreneurship is a process by which citizens build or transform institutions to advance solutions to social problems, such as poverty, illness, illiteracy, environmental destruction, human rights abuses, and corruption.'
>
> —Bornstein & Davis (2010)

A social enterprise is a private entrepreneurial venture built on a promise to contribute to social good. It addresses wicked problems governments continue to grapple with and in sectors/regions where the market mechanism does not find it profitable enough to offer alternatives. Therefore, a social enterprise originates from the entrepreneur's motivation to change through a product or service innovation often made possible using technology. That can range from using an app as a business enabler or embedding AI in the product that attempts to solve a persistent social problem. Social ventures—businesses that pursue profit and social goals simultaneously—have been a sector that has seen tremendous growth in India during the last decade.

Understanding social enterprise business canvas

To understand social enterprises, it is necessary to grasp how they approach three sub-processes of the business model canvas: the value proposition, value creation, and value capture. They differ from commercial ventures in how they look at these processes. Every commercial or social enterprise needs to make enough profits to stay viable. However, their raison d'être is different. Commercial organizations focus on value capture and profit maximization for their shareholders. Social enterprises focus on offering a social value proposition—their purpose is to create value for underserved markets. In addition, there are variations among social enterprises in how they approach value proposition, value creation, and value capture, as we found in our research involving nine leading incubators and social venture funds and thirteen social start-ups from agriculture, education, health, and other sectors.*

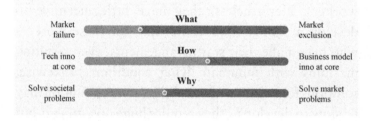

* S. Bhattacharyya et al., 'Report on Start-Up Ecosystem in India', invited chapter, *Innovating for Social Impact: Understanding Innovation, Impact and Support*, (iVEIN Network, IIT Madras, forthcoming).

- *Value Proposition*

Value proposition involves specifying 'what' is the unique contribution that the enterprise aims to deliver. For example, commercial ventures try to articulate value propositions regarding the unmet customer needs they are helping to meet. Social enterprises do this by specifying what social problem they are trying to solve. However, the social issues fall in a spectrum—those arising out of 'market failure' on one end and those arising out of 'market exclusion' on the other.

Market failure refers to situations where problems are left unaddressed as the market players find them lacking in requisite returns or too resource-intensive, making production risky. For example, an enterprise might set up a factory employing several hundred workers. Nevertheless, they have little incentive to develop a proper road or housing for these workers who may make their stay arrangements, even resulting in slums with inhuman living conditions. Likewise, solutions for negative externalities such as pollution may be slow to develop as they require huge investments but cannot be charged to the consumer. Traditionally, the government invests where the market refuses to provide funding for large-scale infrastructure development and sets up high-tech dedicated research institutions for science and technology innovation. Off late, we notice a gradual withdrawal of the government from this role. Social entrepreneurs and social venture funds often fill this institutional void left by the public and corporate sectors. They aid in addressing grand societal challenges and supplement governmental spending for realizing Sustainable Development Goals (SDGs) such as environment, healthcare, and education.

Meghshala is an example of this. Meghshala* is a social enterprise that improves teachers' effectiveness, particularly in government schools, to enhance education quality for the children attending them. Teachers of government schools are often hampered by a lack of practical teaching skills and subject upgradation, and need more resources to make lessons interesting and enjoyable. Meghshala was conceived to help teachers with resource support and an app that mentors them in refining their pedagogy. Its founder, Jyoti Thyagarajan, believes empowering teachers can only transform education. The social venture stepped in to fill the void created by free but low-quality education at government schools, on the one hand, and the expensive alternatives private schools offer in reaching quality education to the most significant number of children.

Market exclusion is a particular kind of market failure. It refers to scenarios where a specific segment of the population—such as the poor or those with physical or mental disabilities, non-binary gender, or Scheduled Caste/Scheduled Tribe status—cannot access resources and opportunities that the general population can

---

* Meghshala, http://meghshala.online/.

access in the open market. Social enterprises attempt to extend market activities to the marginalized and un(der) served, uplifting and empowering them. For example, FIA Technologies offers banking services to the 'unbanked' and the poorest of the poor all across India. Mirakle Couriers run a booming logistics business employing only deaf people.

In reality, market failure and market exclusion do not form an either-or dichotomy; they make more of a continuum. Although some may be closer to one end than the other, social enterprises must balance both in their value propositions. For instance, Kamal Kisan is a social enterprise that designs and manufactures small farm equipment. Historically, agriculture technology development has focused on large farm equipment, which can be sold to large-scale farmers capable of paying for it. This has left a void—a lack of technology solutions for small-scale and marginal farming. By addressing this void, Kamal Kisan can be seen as addressing a market failure. At the same time, it must be noted that their focus is on small-scale and marginal farmers—who make up the most significant proportion of farmers in India—who are extremely poor. They design and deploy their solutions to empower these farmers to increase their productivity and income, thus lifting them out of poverty. Here, Kamal Kisan addresses market exclusion. It does not matter where a social enterprise is in the continuum; what matters is clarity as to where they are.

- *Value Creation*

Value creation pertains to 'how' the enterprise intends to deliver its solution. Commercial enterprises discuss business models and technology innovations as key to providing value. Social enterprises do the same— they use solutions focused on either technology or a business model innovation to solve societal challenges. Some may rely more on technology solutions—such as a prosthetic voice device that enables throat cancer survivors to speak again. The other may focus more on their business model that suits their product/service or enable better customer reach. In either case, given the digital age that we live in, it is taken for granted that all companies may need basic technology solutions involving websites and apps. In a country like India, technology may be pivotal for market access. Technology, in such cases, acts as an enabler for the value proposition rather than a core value creator.

In most cases, technology and business model innovations complement each other in offering innovative solutions and providing a novel route to customers and beneficiaries. Technology must be embedded in the suitable business model for effectiveness because business models help create and capture economic and social value. A business model strategizes how a business identifies stakeholder needs, develops a process of addressing them, reaches the stakeholder, monetizes value, and generates impact.

Technology is often the secret sauce in one or many of these sub-parts of the business model and tends to be deployed differently depending on the enterprise's nature. A case in point is Jyothi Thyagarajan, the founder of Meghshala, a teacher for over thirty years. Even though she had little previous exposure to technology, Jothi realized the power and usefulness of technology to empower and upskill teachers by providing them with well-crafted teaching kits, mentoring, and guidance, turning them into master teachers. Founders from a technology background, like Sneha Priya—from SP Robotics and a winner of national and international competitions in robotics—used robots, AI, VR, and other technologies to boost the creativity and imagination of new-age learners, making technology the backbone of SP Robotics in coaching students build their STEM skills.

Many social entrepreneurs feel they should offer tech-based solutions since 'tech' is in vogue. What matters is if and how technology contributes to solving the problem. Technology development requires heavy investment. Recuperating the tech investment will be challenging for early-stage social enterprises as they struggle to identify revenue streams and wait for them to stabilize. The advice will be—'if a good business model innovation can solve the problem, so be it.' This is not by any means to suggest that social entrepreneurs should stay away from technology—quite the contrary. Many of our complex social and environmental problems badly need deep-tech and deep-science innovations to solve them—but the focus should be on 'appropriate technology', irrespective of the level of complexity.

Innaumation Medical Devices cater to patients who lost their voice when they underwent laryngectomy to treat throat cancer. Aum voice prosthesis, its flagship product, is a low-cost speaking device that helps such people speak again. Dr. Vishal Rao, a renowned surgical oncologist and co-founder of Innaumation, continues to work on core technologies in speech and communication devices, computational biology, and imaging devices to service the underserved. Ameliorate Biotech has developed rapid diagnostic equipment that simultaneously detects malaria, dengue, and chikungunya, the three mosquito-borne diseases rampant in India, for which most primary health centers are not adequately stocked with diagnostic kits. CultYvate has invested in and developed AI and IoT-based farm and crop irrigation solutions in the agri sector to optimize water usage, prevent diseases and pest infestations and increase yield.

In contrast to these deep-tech solutions, SELCO,* which has made technology accessible and affordable to the rural poor, creates low-smoke biomass cookstoves. The stove has helped reduce indoor pollution, decrease

---

* 'Hande for greater use of solar power', *Deccan Herald*, 21 March 2018, https://www.deccanherald.com/content/665782/hande-greater-use-solar-power.html.

firewood use, improve women's and children's health, and save forests. The social enterprise has developed appliances like milking machines, roti rolling machines, and blacksmith fan blowers, to name a few, that create livelihoods.

- *Value Capture*

Value capture signifies 'why' entrepreneurs start their ventures. It denotes what they want out of their efforts. In the case of commercial enterprises, entrepreneurs look for financial returns (in addition to the intrinsic satisfaction of creating a venture of their own). On the other hand, social enterprises are set to bring social and environmental returns to their beneficiaries rather than making a profit for themselves.

Paradoxically, without adequate profits to sustain the business, it is impossible to continue creating social value. Therefore, social ventures continually walk the tightrope, balancing social outcomes for beneficiaries and profits for their sustenance, scale, and growth. Attaining such a balance is tricky, as an increased focus on one would dilute the other. This dissipation of the focus on the beneficiaries results in what is known as 'mission drift', i.e., compromising social goals for financial goals.* As profit margins that a social

---

* A. Ebrahim et al., 'The governance of social enterprises: Mission drift and accountability challenges in hybrid organizations', *Research in Organisational Behavior*, 34 (2014): 81–100.

enterprise makes from the beneficiaries are low, some social enterprises might try to compensate by catering to non-beneficiary customers. Many social enterprises are shifting focus from the 'poorest of the poor' to the 'aspiring middle class' to capture the financial value and stay viable.

Such tensions become more apparent as the enterprise attempts to scale. Interestingly, scaling is essential for widening the social impact and the enterprise's long-term survival. In theory, scaling enables increasing social value capture by expanding the number of beneficiaries and more significant financial value capture thanks to market expansion. In practice, however, the challenge is devising solutions that simultaneously capture social and economic value. For the solutions to work well on the ground, they need to be tailored to a great extent for the beneficiaries. This becomes a hindrance in scaling. For example, agricultural solutions that worked well in northern Karnataka may not work in southern Karnataka, let alone in other states. Moreover, fine-tuning the solutions for each new market segment often stretches young social enterprises' financial and other resources.

The social enterprises that have indeed succeeded in striking the right balance between social and financial value capture are the ones that have created solutions that solve an industry problem along with the social problem. Mirakle Couriers, for instance, has a business model that employs deaf people, a population segment that struggles to get stable and decent-paying jobs. After serving customers including Mahindra & Mahindra, the Aditya Birla Group, Victory Art Foundation, JSW Group, Indian Hotels Company, Godrej & Boyce, and Essel Propack in the past, they now have Amazon as their exclusive customer. Their success is attributed to their creation of a stable and efficient workforce in an industry whose most significant pain point was employee turnover and performance quality.

Social entrepreneurial journey

Becoming a social entrepreneur is an adventurous journey—creating a social enterprise and making sure that the social enterprise scales up in terms of profit and social impact. It has its high points and low points. It is a journey of self-discovery and personal transformation as well. Here, we provide snapshots from the lives and work of various social entrepreneurs to help you visualize it.

• *Getting started—Founder background and inspiration*

Social start-ups offer exciting stories of people, who, moved by a social condition, decided to take the entrepreneurial plunge. Devi Murthy, the founder of Kamal Kisan, is one such. An engineer and business management graduate, Devi realized the difficulties of small farmers when a classmate sought her help designing small farm equipment that would make agricultural operations easier. Small and marginal farmers in India find agriculture unviable due to rising labor costs and their inability to replace labor with off-the-shelf farm equipment that cannot be operated profitably in small, fragmented farms. Devi addressed the gap in the market by interactively designing equipment that reduces dependence on labor while suiting current farming practices and the needs of small farmers.

While Devi had little to do with agriculture, Mallesh Tigali, the founder of CultYvate, came from a farming family. Mallesh recalls with pride how his grandfather, a farmer, could earn more from farming than what his father made in a city. Over the years, however, farm productivity has fallen. The slide in productivity prompted Mallesh to use his technical expertise to develop AI and IoT-based farm and crop irrigation solutions that helped optimize water usage, prevent diseases and pest infestations, and increase yield, making agriculture profitable and sustainable.

Sixty-five-year-old Jyothi Thyagarajan decided to set up Meghshala after thirty years of teaching. Her deep commitment to students from socio-economically weaker sections prompted the founding of Meghshala to solve a real problem of poor-quality education that plagues many a government school. While Jyothi started her venture after retirement, Sneha Priya started SP Robotics when she was barely out of her teens. As a young student, she participated in and won several national and international competitions in robotics. The youngest Iconic Women awardee, Sneha, avows that robots, AI, VR, and other technologies are the best way to boost the creativity and imagination of new-age learners and whet their interest in STEM.

Witnessing the struggles of patients has been the trigger for several healthcare startups. The angst itself, at seeing cancer patients who undergo laryngectomy lose their speech and, subsequently, their jobs and interest in life prompted Dr. Vishal Rao, a renowned surgical oncologist, to think of a solution to give back a voice to those who had lost it. Along with his friend and industrialist, Shashank Mahesh, he co-founded Innaumation Medical Devices, which designed and manufactured cost-effective prosthetic voice boxes. Closer home, losing their eleven-year-old niece to dengue, got the well-experienced duo Dr. Rashbehari Tunga and his wife Dr. Binita S. Tunga on developing a diagnostic device that can successfully detect three mosquito-borne diseases—malaria, dengue, and chikungunya. This early-stage rapid diagnostic kit is a life-saver for rural folks struggling to access remote and underequipped healthcare facilities. While working at the National Centre for Biological Sciences in Bengaluru on therapeutic modalities for breast cancer patients, Dr. Mehrotra noticed a patient who was depressed, too embarrassed to make eye contact, as her breast removal left her feeling incomplete. The psychological trauma she experienced following the mastectomy was worse than the disease. He could not reconcile that hospitals did not offer a solution before or after removing the breast that could have avoided a patient's emotional trauma. Acting on this angst, Dr. Mehrotra quit his job to set up Aarna Biomedical to design and manufacture lightweight, high-quality silicone breast prostheses.

Empathy and environmental consciousness have triggered social entrepreneurship. Witnessing how a simple bus ride could be anxiety-laden for a deaf boy who could not hear the conductor announce the bus stops tugged at Dhruv Lakra's conscience. He resolved to learn sign language and create opportunities for the deaf, who got little public empathy or government assistance in finding employment despite having all the capabilities to work. Dhruv set up Mirakle Couriers and employed deaf people as the work requires only visual skills and no verbal communication. The dissonance between the incredibly high amount of waste we create daily and not finding personal and home care products for a zero-waste living led Sahar Mansoor to set up Bare Necessities. Her background in environmental planning, policy, and law, from Cambridge, and work experience at World Health Organization in Geneva and SELCO Foundation helped form her ideas into an enterprise whose products are free from toxic chemicals and packaging.

- *Finding Co-founders and Implementation Partners*

Social enterprises, in most cases, were set up along with relatives and friends who co-create a solution or acquaintances who turned into partners through a shared vision. For example, Vetrivel Palani, an IT employee, co-founded UzhavarBumi with his brother Paneerselvam to help marginalized farmers earn more by selling fresh milk, milk products, and cold-pressed oils, connecting them to customers through their App—thirty-two micro-entrepreneurs from their dealer network for last-mile delivery. Jyothi Thyagarajan met her co-founder, Sridhar Ranganathan, Founder and CEO of Clood On Inc, at a conference. Ranganathan, a technocrat inspired by her vision of impacting sixty million kids, built the learning management platform hosting Meghshala. Meghshala partners with the governments of Karnataka and Meghalaya, Teach for India, Deshpande Foundation, Makkala Jagriti, Teach Maddi, and Lenovo to reach thousands of teachers.

Anna University alumni Pranavan S. and Sneha Priya became friends and co-founded SP Robotics to teach new-age learners coding, robotics, drones, and virtual reality (VR). More than eighty franchisee partners run their Maker Labs to empower students while being self-employed. While a long-time industrialist friend Shashank Mahesh helped translate Dr. Vishal Rao's idea into a cost-effective prosthetic voice box for their social venture Innaumation, a doctor-couple Dr. Binita

Tunga and Dr. Rashbehari Tunga took their marital partnership further by co-founding Ameliorate Bio-Tech to produce a single device capable of testing three mosquito-borne diseases.

- *Choosing a Legal Structure*

Social enterprises have a social mission like not-for-profit organizations but operate like for-profit companies. They have blurred the boundaries between for-profit and not-for-profit enterprises by combining quality products and services with social benefits and environmental sustainability. In countries such as the US and the UK, such hybridity is recognized with special legal status, and they can choose from a range of legal structures: L3C, social purpose corporations, community interest companies, benefit corporations, etc. Legal structures have a bearing on the funding sources you can tap into. Hybrid structures enable social enterprises to attract non-profit funders such as philanthropists, foundations, aid agencies, and investors such as venture capitalists, angel investors, and private equity funds. For the social entrepreneur, hybrid legal structures also ensure greater autonomy.

India does not have legal structures especially for social enterprises. In India, the legal provision suggested for social enterprises is that of a Section 8 company. This section's key provisions suit organizations devoted to charity, social welfare, environmental protection, and sports-related causes. Though it provides limited liability protection to the founders, it does not allow dividends among its members and profits to be used only to further the business. This probably is why most social enterprises prefer to incorporate themselves as something other than one. A survey by the British Council* revealed that around 60 percent of social enterprises in India operated as private limited companies, 23 percent functioned as an NGO, and only 3 percent chose the Section 8 option.

'A few prosthetic devices can be imported from Europe or the US, but they cost anywhere between Rs 20,000 to Rs 35,000, making them unaffordable for patients from low economic backgrounds. So not being able to pay for a product should not be a reason for anybody not to talk.'
—Shashank Mahesh, co-founder,
Innaumation Medical Devices

Social enterprises choose to be for-profit or not-for-profit, depending on the founders' orientations, funding sources available in the long run, the needs they fulfill, and the socio-economic segments they serve. However, being for-profit does not mean that they are into profiteering. Innaumation Medical Devices set up as a

---

* 'The state of social enterprise in Bangladesh, Ghana, India and Pakistan', British Council, 2016, https://www.britishcouncil.org/sites/default/files/bc-report-ch4-india-digital_0.pdf.

for-profit, retails its voice box for INR 50 while most competitors in the space have priced their product at INR 30,000 upwards up to a lakh. Likewise, Aarna Biomedicals has developed a lightweight silicone prosthesis that is elegant and easy for women who have undergone a mastectomy. Though a for-profit venture, founder Pawan Mehrotra is motivated to provide this as an affordable breast cancer survivor* solution and sells it for as low as INR 4,000.

Similarly, setting up as a non-profit does not mean that the products and services will be free. The social enterprises set up as non-profits seek to generate revenue to self-fund their operations. SELCO, which offers a range of energy products for rural households, follows this approach. However, they ensure the prices are not exploitative and arrange for financial help. Some social enterprises follow pricing models. They may not charge the final beneficiaries but secure the payment from customers who might purchase the product or service on their behalf, such as governments, foundations, or other NGOs.

* *Developing the Technology and Business Model*

Social enterprises tend to work in rural hinterlands, socially and economically marginalized, reaching

---

* Tenzin Norzom, 'This social entrepreneur aims to offer a healthy and affordable breast prosthesis for breast cancer patients', YourStory, 9 December 2020, https://yourstory.com/herstory/2020/12/social-entrepreneur-affordable-breast-prosthesis-cancer.

products and services to the neediest. This requires an enormous effort to understand (sometimes even build) the ecosystem before the products/services can be developed and offered.

Sameer Sawarkar and Rajeev Kumar, both IISc graduates in electronics and communications and colleagues at Motorola, founded Neurosynaptic Communications in 2002 with the vision of making quality and affordable healthcare available in rural India. Their idea was to develop a telemedicine solution for rural areas to provide quality treatment by connecting patients with doctors through video conferencing. The duo spent four years researching rural India to understand consumer expectations and behavior. Primary healthcare facilities needed to be more present or sufficient in most places. Low-quality private players, or even quacks, partially addressed the void.* They found that agrarian beneficiaries in India consider primary healthcare the government's responsibility and expected it for free. They learned that customers were unwilling to pay for a consultation, only for the medicines. Neurosynaptic developed a project-based business model that deployed multiple revenues and delivery models depending on the relevant ecosystem being addressed.

---

* Rema Nagarajan, 'Are 57% 'doctors' quacks? Govt says no, then yes', *Times of India*, 9 August 2019, https://timesofindia. indiatimes.com/india/are-57-docs-quacks-govt-says-no-then-yes/ articleshow/70596627.cms.

Their first solution involved a telemedicine platform that worked online but needed low bandwidth and consumed little power. Their follow-up studies showed that consultation over the telemedicine platform alone would not create better health outcomes. Often the doctors suggested diagnostic tests, which were not locally available, and people were reluctant to travel elsewhere to get them done. So Sameer and Rajeev developed highly sophisticated diagnostic devices that kiosk operators can administer without medical training. They had to also think of the misuse of these devices, for example, by the quacks; there had to be safeguarded in place (like network permissions to use the system) to ensure safe usage.

They needed implementation partners to use the diagnostic devices, but trained personnel were hard to find. It was an uphill task to find reliable and trained partners who would be acceptable to the people (women and children would not prefer a male technician). Further, the kiosks had to be set up at places that were accessible and perceived to be safe for women and children to visit.

- *Co-creating an Ecosystem*

Setting up a social enterprise with a new business model requires an ecosystem allowing enterprises to operate and grow their business. Some social enterprises are so pathbreaking that they must create such an ecosystem. An enabling institutional environment requires appropriate technological, legal, and regulatory infrastructure.*

When Neurosynaptic entered the field, the ecosystem was very nascent. The founders then had to decide whether to wait for the ecosystem to develop or develop it themselves. They chose the latter. Several social enterprises have had a bumpy start to their journey, creating a supportive institutional environment. In 2002, when Neurosynaptic started, telemedicine was being used only sparingly, and that too just for secondary, tertiary/specialist care. Specialists from premier healthcare institutions would be contacted over communication technology platforms for advice in complicated medical situations by doctors in remote regions who could not transport the patient. For instance, the doctor treating an accident victim in Andaman might contact specialists at AIIMS to decide on the line of treatment to be administered instead of flying the patient over to them. This was done with the help of satellite connectivity through a free network set up by ISRO that was available throughout India, connecting leading hospitals, a facility that still exists. However, this was not a network that would work for what Neurosynaptic had in mind. So they had to develop the technology that would work with the standard phone

---

* 'Building enabling ecosystems for social enterprises Brussels, 22-23 April 2015', moderator's report, Capacity Building Seminar, https://www.oecd.org/cfe/leed/CBS-ecosystem-22-23-Apr15-Sum-report.pdf.

lines. They used a low bandwidth communication protocol developed in IIT Madras as the base to build their telemedicine platform.

Similarly, there was no legal/regulatory framework concerning the use of telemedicine in primary healthcare in 2002. In 2003, the Department of Information Technology, Ministry of Communications and Information Technology, issued the Recommended Guidelines & Standards for Practice of Telemedicine, which only suggest how telemedicine would be practiced. However, in the wake of the Covid-19 pandemic, the Ministry of Health and Family Welfare issued guidelines allowing registered medical practitioners to consult and treat patients using telemedicine. Likewise, standards and protocols for trying some diagnostic devices were also absent. Sameer and Rajeev had to work with doctors and hospitals to develop relevant protocols.

The Government of India took up ecosystem development earnestly by introducing social enterprise development programs in the 12th FYP of 2012–17 to foster inclusive and sustainable growth. 'The Decade of Innovation', implemented by the Indian government, attempted to develop innovative solutions at the lowest cost possible through strategies and policy guidelines to establish an ecosystem of capacity building around BoP solutions. The National Innovation Council was given a ten-year window (2010–20) to set up facilities, guide the discussions, and analyze and implement inclusive innovation strategies.

Today, social enterprises led by technology-driven and socially responsible leaders have developed viable models to build a sustainable future. The timing is now right to effectively address the complex developmental needs with market-based models and socially conscious stewardship. With many incubators and accelerators there to guide and support social entrepreneurs, this is the best time to try out innovative solutions for long-standing social and environmental challenges.

8

Getting a Social Enterprise off the Ground: Understanding the Funding and Incubation Landscape

'Go outside your home and see the coconut vendor or the chai walla (tea seller). They are bootstrapped. So, if you don't overthink it, you realize that if the chai walla is in business, maybe I can be in business too without outside money.'

—Sridhar Vembu, Founder, Zoho

~

Resources primarily come from within the organization in Corporate Social Responsibility and Corporate Social Innovation. A social entrepreneur who steps out of the corporate boundary will have to fetch these resources from the external business ecosystem independently. It can look very daunting to an aspiring social entrepreneur. However, knowing the funding and incubation landscape closer might help make the best use of what is available. In this chapter, we discuss various funding options available to social ventures to lay bare the advantages and appropriateness of each of them. We pay special attention to impact investors and their role in supporting social enterprises. We then briefly discuss the incubation landscape as well.

Funding sources

Social enterprises can choose funding sources depending on how they incorporate their company and the stage of their growth. In the case of an early-stage social venture, **bootstrapping** is the most common funding source—it involves deploying founders' resources that include personal savings or money earned from a second job and plowing back a part of the revenue. Bootstrapping becomes necessary as most funders must see business traction before investing. The most significant advantage of bootstrapping is that it helps the entrepreneur retain control over the business and is not bogged down by interest burden. However, it is essential to remember that equity investments take away part ownership of the company, and too much exposure can heavily curtail strategic and operational freedom. Another slice of bootstrapping is the 'sweat equity' or the non-monetary contributions like time and effort invested by the entrepreneur in the venture. As the company grows, sweat equity becomes a part of what can be monetized during an acquisition or funding through investors' equity. Hence, business owners must keep track of all their monetary and non-monetary contributions to the company.

When bootstrapping becomes inadequate to finance the growing venture, the recourse is usually **friends and family**, an extension of bootstrapping. It can be in the form of a gift, a loan, or equity. This funding source comes with the advantage of the funder's faith in the founder and the idea, which is not dependent on market indicators. Further, the terms of the loans are usually less stringent and can be renegotiated easily. However, entrepreneurs need to carefully assess personal risk using this funding source as a failed business can ruin personal relations and socially isolate them.

As the enterprise develops its product/service, it will need more prototyping and testing in the market. The product development process involves five steps: brainstorming and ideation, research and idea screening, concept development, prototyping and evaluation, and product rollout and iteration. Research and development grants are the most sought-after funding source at the ideation and prototyping stage. Not-for-profit enterprises must rely on grants and donations as the primary funding source throughout their lifecycle. The World Bank, US Aid, Action Aid, Asian Development Bank, Bill and Melinda Gates Foundation, and philanthropy-based impact investors like Omidyar Network are a few among many. Technopreneur Promotion Program (TePP) from the Department of Science and Technology, Government of India, Multiplier Grants Scheme presented by the Department of Electronics and Information Technology, the 10,000 Startups program by NASSCOM, Unlimited India, Zone Startup, Amity Innovation Incubators, and Amrita TBI in partnership with Government of India are some of the noteworthy grant providers in the social innovation space. Though popular, as grant money need not be paid back, preparing grant proposals can take time, often with long waiting periods and uncertain outcomes. Once grants are received, the enterprise will need to monitor and report periodically to the granting agency and ensure the achievement of impact indicators.

A few interim options help raise capital until the enterprise is ready for more significant investments. **Business plan competitions**, social enterprise challenges, and case competitions are all excellent avenues for initial though small funding, with the added advantage of getting noticed by angel investors. In addition, Upaya Social Ventures, Unitus Seed Fund, Impact Circle, and Indian Angel Network offer early-stage funding.

Indiatech HK, Climate Launchpad, and Eximius are business-plan competitions that have offered entrepreneurs a platform to showcase their innovative startup ideas. They are all associated with big brand investment partners and community partners like IndiaGoesGlobal, a platform that helps early-stage startups grow sustainably. In addition, the government encourages new entrepreneurs to develop innovative deep-tech products through the Atal New Innovation Mission and its business plan competition—Atal New India Challenge. The competition, through its grant, supports commercializing deep tech in the Indian context. The ministries that fund and support the startups selected from the competition are Agriculture and Farmers' Welfare, Railways, Road Transport and Highways, Housing and Urban Affairs, and Drinking Water and Sanitation. The startups are to ideate and create innovative novel solutions for the ministries' various challenges.

Entrepreneurship cells of premier institutions also conduct business plan competitions.*The prominent among them are Conquest (BITS Pilani) and Eureka! (IIT Bombay), Vishishth (IIT Delhi), Uddyam (SP Jain), Ventura (NIT Trichy), IIIT Allahabad B-Plan Competition, and Empresario (IIT Kharagpur). Besides offering mentoring opportunities to fine-tune their business plan, such competitions are a platform to meet and pique the interest of angel investors, venture capitalists, and industry leaders.

Crowdfunding is gaining popularity and can test out early-stage projects, gain visibility by introducing the idea to the market, and sometimes even pre-

---

* 'Top business plan competitions in India to participate for Start-ups', BizzBucket, 24 February 2020, https://bizzbucket.co/business-plan-competitions-in-india/.

sell.* Crowdfunding enables a social entrepreneur to gather small amounts of funds from many individuals. Such an opportunity also creates high visibility in the virtual world. The widespread usage of social media and digital payments has made it possible to raise funds through crowdsourcing platforms.† For social ventures, popular crowdfunding platforms like Milaap, ImpactGuru, Ketto, Fueladream, and Dreamwallets connect social entrepreneurs and NGOs to potential investors expediently and efficiently. Two advantages of crowdfunding have democratized funding opportunities. First, is the right way of building a community of supporters for the product or service. Second, is the dramatically improved chances of women entrepreneurs getting funding.‡

For-profit social enterprises can seek funds from **angel investors** and **venture capitalists** in return for equity to achieve scale and impact. Angels are early-stage investors who pitch in with funds when a social

---

* 'Crowdfunding is a great way for new businesses to test the waters before launching product, going big', *Financial Express*, 21 October 2020, https://www.financialexpress.com/industry/sme/cafe-sme/msme-fin-crowdfunding-is-a-great-way-for-new-businesses-to-test-the-waters-before-launching-product-going-big/2110545/.

† Roshni Balaji, '5 crowdsourcing platforms to help you raise funds for social good in a jiffy', YourStory, 9 February 2020, https://yourstory.com/socialstory/2020/02/crowdsourcing-platforms-funds-ngo-social.

‡ 'The Ultimate Introductory Guide to Funding Your Social Enterprise', Acumen Academy, https://acumenacademy.org/blog/impact-capital-funding-your-social-enterprise.

enterprise has to build organizational capability with a sales and marketing team and streamline the supply chain and logistics to reach the market. Though the business idea may be well-formed, building organizational capacity requires fresh investments, which the angels provide. Angel investors fund the riskiest phase of social enterprise growth. The most significant infusion is money, strategic advice, and connection to networks that can help the business grow and provide credibility for the venture. Angel investors fund a venture by buying shares at an agreed price that will later be sold when the company has developed or been acquired. As the investment is made at a very risky stage, angels expect higher returns for their investment. Generally, they invest in several new ventures at a time. Being an angel, they do not expect interest on money invested or year-on-year dividends for their investments. The choice of an angle needs to include a match in vision of the enterprise founder, as a lack of alignment is likely to result in clashes in the enterprise's strategic direction and operational strategies: entrepreneurs, founders of unicorns, and professionals who have headed companies make up most angel investors in India.

An established enterprise with a well-laid-out business model, first-rate product-to-market fit with a foothold in the market, and looking to scale up will seek venture funds for a fund infusion. Venture fund investments in social enterprises aim to further innovations, create deep social impact and are usually a sizeable pot of money invested. Many venture capitalists are sector agnostic. They prefer enterprises operating in rural or semi-urban areas to build sustainable businesses and empower the poor and marginalized. They generally expect a ten-fold return on capital when the company is sold or goes for an IPO.[*] Social Alpha, Villgro, Caspian, Lok Capital, Unitus Capital, and Acumen are top venture funds supporting India's social enterprises.[†]

In case enterprise founders are not keen on relinquishing even part of control over their firm, then **debt funds** are a good option. Debt funds come in the form of term loans that need to be serviced in full, along with interest. Many times debts need to be secured with assets of the enterprise. However, debt funds are to be resorted to only when the short-term revenue stream is in place.

The Government of India has provisioned several funding sources for social ventures. **The Samridhi Fund** by the Small Industries Development Bank of India (SIDBI) provides risk capital to scalable enterprises working on economic, social, or environmental causes for the poor in eight low-income states of Rajasthan Uttar Pradesh, Madhya Pradesh, Bihar, Chhattisgarh,

---

[*] Ibid.

[†] Urvi Jacob, '[2020 outlook] Here are 7 social impact VCS to look out for this year', YourStory, 10 January 2020, https://yourstory.com/socialstory/2020/01/2020-outlook-social-impact-vcs-india.

Jharkhand, Odisha, and West Bengal. Using equity and convertible instrument, the fund offers growth capital to growth-stage companies with an innovative sound business model, products, and technologies ready for increasing scale. INR 5–25 crores are provided for social ventures that provide water and sanitation solutions, affordable healthcare, agriculture and allied services, clean energy, financial inclusion, and skill-building. In addition, the government encourages innovation and dynamic enterprises to solve problems in the economic pyramid base through The India Inclusive Innovation Fund, the Venture Capital Fund for Scheduled Castes, India Opportunities Venture Fund, and the Kisan Credit Card Scheme.

Impact investment: Funds for social transformations

Global Impact Investing Network (GIIN) defines impact investing as 'investment that generates positive, measurable social and environmental transformation besides financial returns'.* GIIN offers three core characteristics of impact investing. They are:

• Investing to support a social venture that will have a positive impact and environmental sustainability.

---

* 'What you need to know about impact investing', Global Impact Investing Network, https://thegiin.org/impact-investing/need-to-know/#what-is-impact-investing.

- Impact investors expect lower returns from their investment in social ventures. The returns from impact investing are of three levels—risk-adjusted and comparable to market rate are the most common. Below market rate but closer to it and below market rate and closer to the capital protection are the other less deployed levels.
- Assistance is provided through a range of asset classes—cash to fixed income, venture capital, and private equity.

It is evident that impact investing intertwines charitable objectives with mainstream financial decision-making. Two principles form the core of impact investment: the blended value principle and sustainable financial return. While the blended value necessitates social businesses to achieve economic and social returns, sustainable financial returns require financial returns to be sufficient for long-term viability.

Several angel investors and venture funds who support social enterprises that can offer a positive social impact and financial returns, call themselves 'Impact Investors'. Synonyms like value-based investing, socially responsible investment, sustainable investing, patient capital, mission-driven funding, and blended value* describe this form of financing.

---

* 'Impact investments and social enterprises', India Global Business, https://indiaincgroup.com/impact-investments-social-enterprises/.

Impact investors also claim to have tempered return expectations and are patient in exit periods. The focus of impact investors is sustainable agriculture, clean energy, environmental conservation, healthcare, water and sanitation, affordable housing, skilling, and livelihood expansion programs.

The impetus for impact investing in India comes from the high levels of income inequities in the country. According to an Oxfam International Report,[*] in 2017, the top 10 percent of Indians owned 77 percent of the nation's wealth. During the same period, 67 million Indians could increase their wealth by a paltry 1 percent. With government investments in priority sectors like primary education, healthcare, affordable housing, and insufficient water and sanitation to close the disparity gap, private investors have enough room to step in and help bridge the chasm. Impact investing can be a vehicle for private funds to move into the social sector. Impact investors can deliver enormous impact by supplanting funds and business management practices into the social sector.

The last fifteen years have witnessed impact investments gaining ground in India, now globally known as the 'epicenter of impact investing'[†]

---

[*] 'India: extreme equality in numbers', Oxfam International, https://www.oxfam.org/en/india-extreme-inequality-numbers.

[†] A. Rajan et al., 'The Global Epicenter of Impact Investing: An Analysis of Social Venture Investments in India', *Journal of Private Equity*, (2014): 37–50.

and 'impact lab of the world'.* Through impact investments, private capital has been channeled into social and environmental causes, bridging resource gaps that mar India's progress on achieving the Sustainable Development Goals. The government and developmental financial institutions were the primary investors of social or environmental initiatives—the micro-finance boom of the 2000s pumped private money into enterprises that targeted the BoP segment. Perhaps the setting up of Avishkar, the first for-profit Indian Impact Fund, and the entry of Acumen, the global impact investment player, into India, both in 2001, marked the official beginnings of the entry of foreign investments in India.

The Impact Investors Council (IIC), an industry body working towards strengthening the industry, currently has twenty-eight members (IIC website). According to the Venture Intelligence databases (which cover only equity investments), 115+ firms have invested in social startups in the past five years. Further, philanthropies and foundations (e.g., Michael and Susan Dell Foundation) have entered the space with funding instruments such as returnable grants and outcome-based-debt.† Traditional private

---

* 'Annual Impact Investor Survey 2020', Global Impact Investing Network, June 2020, https://thegiin.org/assets/GIIN%20 Annual%20Impact%20Investor%20Survey%202020.pdf.
† Shamika Ravi et al., 'The promise of impact investing in India', Brookings Institution India Center, July 2019.

investors are also lending to social ventures. Each of these investors has varying approaches in funding and risk-return-impact orientations, leading to definitional confusion as to who an impact investor is in India's context.

Reports by IIC share a largely positive story of impact investing, with impact investors graduating from providing Seed and Series A funding to providing funding for later stages of enterprise development, increasing ticket sizes, and average rates of returns that beat market rates.* They report that most exits between 2010–15 have met or exceeded market rates of return, with the top one-third having a median MRR of 34 percent and an average exit time of 4.9 years.[†] Impact investors also are said to have gone way beyond their role as investors by providing active handholding to the investee enterprises.[‡] Impact investments have grown almost 200 percent from USD 650 million in 2016 to USD 1.7 billion by 2019.

However, research studies[§] on impact investors and social enterprises reveal a somewhat stifled

* Ibid.
[†] Vivek Pandit and Toshan Tamhane, 'Impact investing: Purpose-driven finance finds its place in India', McKinsey & Company, September 2017.
[‡] Shamika Ravi et al., 'The promise of impact investing in India', Brookings Institution India Center, July 2019.
[§] 'Annual Impact Investor Survey 2020', Global Impact Investing Network, June 2020, https://thegiin.org/assets/GIIN%20Annual%20Impact%20Investor%20Survey%202020.pdf.

relation between the two arising from mismatched expectations. Our recent research throws light on where such mismatches arise.

- *Impact investor categories*

All impact investors are not the same in their expectations. There was an increasing sense of ambivalence about the fundamental nature and true intentions of the varied actors who now called themselves 'impact investors'. Though several new entrants professed to seek a blended value of financial and social returns while creating a sustainable growth model from their investee social startups, some were indistinguishable from mainstream venture capitalists. A probable reason for this blurring of distinction is the slackening of the drive for impact and increased motivation to earn commercial VC-level returns. This trend is problematic because impact investors are moving closer to the traditional private equity model rather than the other way, diluting the real purpose of impact investing. For many, the impact becomes secondary and is often traded off for financial returns. Some commercial investors are co-opting the impact of investor identity. As a result, the more socially-oriented investors now do not want to be called impact investors. Instead, they differentiate themselves as patient investors to convey their philosophy and approaches.

- *Focal sectors, geographies, and beneficiaries*

Impact investors vary in their preferences for industry sectors, geographies, and the beneficiaries they invest in. These variations indicate whether an impact investor is more oriented toward social impact or financial returns.

Surprisingly, we found many impact investors to be more risk-averse than the mainstream venture capitalists and therefore prefer to invest in sectors where they are sure of returns. Agriculture, education, and healthcare are the most favored sectors, and investments are being made in technology-based ventures across sectors. Technology-based ventures are widely believed to scale quickly in a large market like India and fetch early or higher returns. Resultantly, several social ventures present themselves as 'tech' companies when the only technology they deploy is an app for customer interface. While we see investments shifting toward tier 1 and 2 towns, most were still made in metros, predominantly in southern, northern, and western India. The safe playing impact investors still needed to find entrepreneurs from smaller towns and villages.

Impact investors are often reluctant to invest in specific sectors and geographies that they consider challenging to create business models that sustainably generate revenues. In actuality, the hesitation is due to the intended beneficiaries—the marginalized, underprivileged, and excluded groups who are often unable to pay even a paltry amount for services. Such an inability to pay makes value capture challenging, driving away some impact investors. For them, the beneficiary customers' revenue potential was foundational to the investee business models' sustainability. We find impact investors expanding their target beneficiary population. From the earlier conceptualization of beneficiaries as BoP and/or unserved segments, some impact investors have now moved on to the 'missing middle'. Their focus was a growing underserved group of beneficiaries who had graduated from the BoP level and yet could not access affordable finance, good education, or quality healthcare. Impact investors have made a pragmatic shift of focus to social enterprises catering to the next rung above the BoP, as this beneficiary segment can pay for services.

- *Investment approaches*

Impact investors vary widely in their preferred deal sizes and exit periods, creating a funding gap for aspiring social enterprises. Thanks to the transactional costs and regulatory hurdles in concluding funding deals, many impact investors now prefer to do fewer deals but larger ticket sizes. The exit is often decided early based on the social startup's exhibited potential. We found that venture funds exited profitable companies if they could not achieve growth. Patient investors, on the contrary, believe that a ten-year investment window is essential for achieving impact. Therefore, it would be worthwhile for financial institutions to reflect on the merits of long-term funding and develop a range of appropriate financial products to aid sustainable growth.

Social venture funds in India

The Alternative Investment Funds (AIF) Regulations enacted by SEBI in 2012 introduced the concept of 'social venture funds', a vehicle for pooling funds from Indian and foreign investors for investing based on a pre-decided social impact policy.

NGOs, high-net-worth individuals, and companies who want to invest their CSR funds in social enterprises can set up an SVF. Social venture funds invest primarily in securities or units of social ventures that operate within the ambit of social performance norms laid down by the fund. In return, investors earn limited returns. Such social venture funds differ from venture capital funds and private equity funds in investments they make and their expected returns. Firstly, they offer grants for social impact rather than a return on investment. When investing through equity, they expect par or below-par returns instead of venture funds' high IRR expectations in equity investments. Secondly, they make long-term investments in socially, environmentally conscious companies that positively impact the geographies where the portfolio companies operate. Finally, the

SVF management team actively mentors and grows its portfolio companies, increasing investments when the company grows.

Since the core intentionality is to bring about a positive impact, measuring impact is vital. Therefore, the investment process needs to chart out best practices to set targets, measure performance on those matrices, and report success in achieving the target outcomes.

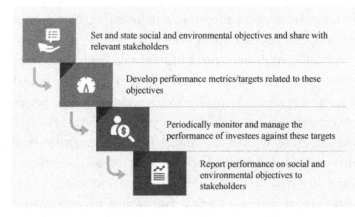

Impact Assessment Framework: GIIN*

In conclusion, there are myriad options to find funding for social entrepreneurship. The Union Ministry of Finance recently announced the setting up a social stock

---

* 'What you need to know about impact investing', Global Impact Investing Network, https://thegiin.org/impact-investing/need-to-know/#what-is-impact-investing.

exchange (SSE) in India. The purpose is to raise capital for organizations working for the realization of a social welfare objective.* Further, eight environmental, social, and corporate governance (ESG) mutual funds have been launched in India. In its Union budget, the government has underscored its focus on six social development pillars. These pillars are health and well-being, physical and financial capital, infrastructure, inclusive development, reinvigorating human capital and innovation, research, and development.† These initiatives are bound to boost the social sector further with the release of new and ample funding.

Incubation landscape

Incubators and accelerators are essential components of the startup ecosystem. They provide entrepreneurs with resources by supporting them with ideas and network connections to fine-tune their business plans and product offering. In addition, by providing mentoring and access to networks, incubators become a go-to destination for fledgling enterprises to start on

---

* Ishan Kukreti, 'Economic Survey 2021 backs setting up of Social Stock Exchange in India', *Down to Earth*, 30 January 2021, https://www.downtoearth.org.in/news/economy/economic-survey-2021-backs-setting-up-of-social-stock-exchange-in-india-75276.
† 'Union Budget 2021 explained in 15 charts', *Times of India*, 1 February 2021, https://timesofindia.indiatimes.com/business/india-business/union-budget-2021-explained-in-15-charts/articleshow/80631848.cms.

the right foot and grow rapidly. Several also offer co-working spaces and a cohort of other entrepreneurs to share and learn.

Though considered the same, incubators and accelerators are meant for different stages of an enterprise's journey and work toward different outcomes. Incubators are ideally meant for ideation and business plan development. On being incubated, a social startup can refine its idea, build its business plan and work on product-market fit. Further, they can identify and work on intellectual property issues and build networks in the ecosystem. There is no set period within which these outcomes are to be achieved. The incubator gets a percentage of the company's equity.

Accelerators select and work with early-stage startups who are likely to benefit most from their support. Startups that already have a set business plan and product and need mentorship and support to scale up. They often encourage startups to find their space. Still, they offer a host of facilities, including guest lectures by established entrepreneurs, policymakers, and investors to whom pitches can be made. Accelerators have a stricter selection process, often selecting just 10 percent of the applicants. The selected applicants are given a fixed period of a few months to acquire and utilize high-quality support. The choice between joining an incubator or an accelerator depends on the startup's growth stage. Incubator support would be valuable if they are in the early stage of developing the product or business plan and testing out the market. An accelerator could facilitate the next growth spurt if the enterprise is ready with a minimum viable product (MVP stage).

Indian incubation ecosystem has rapidly grown in the last decade with the entry of new public and private sector incubators and accelerators. There are a few among them that focus exclusively on social enterprises. Social enterprises, particularly tech startups, would get a fillip in their early stages when incubated by technology incubators like Rural Technology and Business Incubator (RTBI) set up by IIT Madras. Social startups working on rural businesses and those using information and communication technologies in high-impact sectors like livelihoods, agriculture, financial inclusion, etc., are preferred for incubation support like initial funding, mentoring, and network access. Similarly, the Centre for Innovation, Incubation, and Entrepreneurship at IIM Ahmedabad supports social startups by connecting them to investors, developmental agencies, mentors, and corporates. Villgro has a 100-day incubation plan during which startups are trained in technical skills, human resources, and financial management and helped to develop go-to-market strategies. Social Alpha's unique focus is deep-tech social enterprises that address a select set of grand societal challenges.

Getting support from incubators and accelerators

Incubators and accelerators undertake a multi-stage selection process to select the social startup they are prepared to support. They all have a set of criteria that they apply in the selection process. Having a good understanding of them will increase your chances of securing support. Our research with the incubators and accelerators in India found them looking at the following aspects in their decision-making process.

* *Problem and beneficiary characteristics:* The incubators/accelerators diverged in their preference for the problems they sought to address and, consequently, the intended beneficiary characteristics. Even though several of them strictly focused on beneficiaries who were economically marginalized/BoP population, the criteria for determining what the BoP consisted of varied. They would favor a social enterprise only if they aimed to solve the problems of their interest, generating social impact among their target beneficiary segments.
* *Impact type:* While the nature of the solutions that the social enterprises (product innovations, service or business-model innovations, technology as a core or enabler) offered varied, the difference that mattered was the type of impact. Some incubators/

accelerators were focused on social enterprises offering solutions that improved incomes, assets, and livelihoods for the poor.

- *Scalability:* The solution's scalability was a parameter used to judge the financial viability of the social enterprise and its ability to generate social impact in the long run.

- *Firm stage:* While there was a wide disparity in the preferred venture stage to step in with support, the incubators/accelerators focusing on product innovation accepted seed-stage startups even at the idea or proof-of-concept stage. Those focusing on livelihood-generating business models preferred later-stage companies.

- *Financial sustainability:* Applicants were selected based on their business model's viability. Financial sustainability and scalability were imperative for most, though minimal to modest returns were accepted, as the primary goal was impact rather than profit.

- *Entrepreneur characteristics:* Entrepreneurial motivation was a crucial criterion across the board. Many were careful not to accept social entrepreneurs prone to 'incubator hopping'. Some actively sought out entrepreneurs outside the English-speaking demographics to promote grassroots social enterprises. Intangible capabilities such as team dynamics and sectoral knowledge were deemed significant parameters for selection.

Once a startup is chosen to be incubated, social impact indicators and financials are used as parameters to monitor their progress. While global tools such as IRIS were the industry standard to measure social impact, most impact investors used their in-house tools to track impact. While the breadth measures tracked the number of beneficiaries impacted, the depth measures tried to map how deeply the beneficiaries' lives were affected by changes. Monitoring of venture financials, in comparison, was mainly a routine matter. A common refrain was that the prevalent matrix of evaluating and evaluating startups was inappropriate for social ventures. Even though the social impact was considered more crucial than financial viability, no premium was attached to it during valuation. Further, most primarily focused on the business's cash flows to assess financial health and venture sustainability. Social companies had to be profitable enough to self-sustain, though not essentially earn high returns.

Part 5

Embarking on the Journey

'*Wanderer, there is no path. You lay a path in walking.*'
—*A. Machado*

9

Becoming an Impact
Champion: An Action Plan

This concluding chapter summarizes the salient ideas
illustrated and explained in the book. The flow of the
chapter, therefore, mirrors the book's organization.
Finally, we list the action points and management
tools that can aid you in being an Impact Champion
and, more importantly, guide you in incorporating the
ideals of social value creation, social benefit, and social
advancement in organizational and business processes.

Social consciousness: The imperative of
our times

As an Impact Champion, your role is to convince your
company that as they conduct their business in a socio-
economic ecosystem, it is imperative to be sensitive to
the expectations of a more extensive set of stakeholders
rather than just the shareholders. In addition, you

will champion the processes of embedding social consciousness as an underlying value that guides organizational mission, planning, and operations. Ultimately, social consciousness would align with corporate and societal interests.

Action Point 1

As an Impact Champion, you will act as an intrapreneur committed to using business as a powerful force for doing good within your organization and one who is not afraid of stepping out and taking on the role of an entrepreneur for creating a social enterprise that will tackle a wicked problem if you feel constrained by organizational boundaries.

CORE VALUES

Act with care

Be truthful

Be honest

Use discretion

Avoid personal greed

Your action plan as a social intrapreneur should be executed through the following steps:

- Identify and communicate the normative values of concern for people (employees and external stakeholders), sustainability, and the environment. Gain the agreement of the senior management for the same.

- Translate the organizational mission statement and goals into a language understandable and executable by all employees.
- Disseminate the mission and goals widely within the organization.
- Dialogue with employees to align organizational goals with sustainability and environmental preservation.
- Initiate dialogue in an atmosphere of psychological safety wherein ideas can be challenged and co-created with employees to achieve the mission.
- Choose a pathway for achieving the goals concerning sustainability and environmental management.
- Set up internal systems to implement social responsibility, like a CSR committee of interested employees and a business innovation cell that encourages socially valuable innovations.
- Role model and encourage employees to volunteer their time and efforts for social responsibility projects through the vehicle of CSR.
- Advocate evaluation of any new business or product innovation from the social and sustainability dimension. This will help convert social consciousness into societal accomplishments.
- Work with HR in reinforcing a robust value-centered organizational culture.

Society and development: Corporate partnering for equitable and sustainable growth

The easiest way for your company to contribute to SDGs is by aligning your CSR activities with SDGs. Achieving SDGs will need the active participation of the private sector, government NGOs, and civic society. As an Impact Champion, you are the bridge connecting these different stakeholder groups.

Action Point 2: Being a Social Intrapreneur

As an Impact Champion, you must convince management of the strategic importance of contributing to SDGs through CSR projects and business innovations. You would also initiate your company into cross-sector partnerships that can work together on specific SDGs.

Your internal advocacy will be exercised through two pathways:

Corporate Social Responsibility and its alignment with SDGs

- Check for all the ongoing CSR projects and work with the CSR manager in mapping them to the SDGs.
- Identify SDGs that align with your company's mission and goals.
- Brainstorm new CSR project areas and ideas that will align with the chosen set of SDGs.

- Identify and build connections with external stakeholders who have expertise in specific areas of intervention like wastewater treatment and recycling, maternal healthcare, or disability audit of infrastructure.
- Ensure updating the corporate website to indicate SDGs connected to your business.
- Indicate how your company is helping to advance them, directly or indirectly.

Corporate Social Innovations advancing SDGs

- Business leaders need to translate SDGs into corporate goals and targets.
- Initiate business and/or technology innovations to achieve the SDG targets.
- Track the progress diligently.
- Make the results public.

Corporate Social Responsibility: Giving back to society

Your first foray into working on social responsibility can be through corporate social responsibility. Consider your company's competitive strengths and identify potential areas that can be developed into an integral part of your CSR. The actions leading to a robust CSR program should involve employees across levels. Your role as an Impact Champion will involve advocacy across three levels to convey employee role expectations throughout the organization.

Action Point 3: Role Expectations that You Need to Convince Your Colleagues across Your Company

Top management:
- Sharpen organizational focus and strategy for CSR
- Select areas of CSR contribution that are core to the expertise of the organization
- Ensure internal business processes positivley imapct society
- Establish transparent and sustainble SR initiatives that convey a shared vision with local communities and society

Doing your bit

Manager of teams:
- Encourage employee volunteering for CSR projects
- Being a role model to team members
- Use CSR for internally branding the organizational

Individual performer:
- Volunteering in CSR project teams
- Taking initiative to start and sustain locally relevant social responsiblity initiatives
- Speak about the satisfaction derived from volunteering experiences

Social Impact Assessment: An essential tool to ensure actual impact

Implementing Section 135 has further enhanced corporate contributions as part of social responsibility. However, in the seven years of mandatory CSR, most companies have yet to progress from merely reporting their CSR activities. As an Impact Champion, you need to ensure the social return on your company's investments, both in CSR and corporate social innovations.

Action Point 4: Adopting a Proactive Stance for Continually Improving Developmental Outcomes of CSR and CSI Projects

You can measure social impact by answering the following questions:

- Are the initiatives that have been launched, CSR or CSI (or Social Entrepreneurship when you start your social enterprise), generating the societal benefit they promise?
- Are they bringing about the changes that they had envisioned?
- Can they improve their reach?
- How can their impact be enhanced?

Social Impact Assessment will require you to:

- Clarify the difference between objectives, inputs, outcomes, and impact within the organizations and important stakeholders.
- Differentiate social projects in terms of their target beneficiaries. Micro-level beneficiaries (for example, school students) or meso-level

beneficiaries (schools in a district) will require different measurement metrics.

- Assess impact at various points in the project timeline—before the beginning of the project, on completing the project, assessing halfway through a project for a medium-term review, and after a few years to assess the lasting impact.
- Measure the breadth and depth of social impact.
- Measure long-term impact at the individual-enterprise-ecosystem level.
- Use a multidimensional and multi-level framework for impact assessment—the multiple dimensions are human capital, financial resources, physical amenities, social capital, and awareness of political rights. The individual beneficiary, family, and community are the three levels at which impact is assessed.
- Develop measurement metrics for capturing return on investment and the multiplier effect of the spending on various beneficiaries.

Corporate Social Innovation: Widening the scope of corporate innovation

By daring the corporates to expand their focus to people and the planet, CSI would enable steering corporate creativity and innovations to address pressing social and environmental issues. Corporates today appreciate the specific circumstances and challenges facing different stakeholder groups.

Action Point 5: As an Impact Champion, You Must Take Up the Challenge of Devising Innovative Means to Create Value for Different Stakeholder Groups.

- Champion a circular economy—one that is regenerative and restorative by design. Replace the prevalent linear model with a circular approach to the use of resources.
- Focus on circular production systems that incorporate reuse, repair, refurbishment, remanufacturing, and recycling in the production process to reduce the need for new resources and waste creation.
- Encourage creating in-house designs to reduce the use of resources to the minimum and generate only a minimal amount of waste and pollutants.
- Urge reuse, repair, refurbishment, and recycling possibilities to the maximum in manufacturing.
- In pricing models, consider 'sharing' models rather than 'ownership' models.
- Avoid using non-renewable resources and rely on renewable ones—incorporate processes for replenishing the natural resources in the production system and business models.

- Include environment-related targets among the corporate goals.
- Reduce carbon footprint, use renewable energy sources, reduce plastic and other waste, regenerate soil and water sources, etc.
- Actively track the progress on reducing the carbon footprint and share them with the broader stakeholders.
- Introduce and encourage a radical rethinking of the existing designs and business models, investment, and deeper-level changes in organizational functioning.

Championing Corporate Social Innovation: How it is done

Creating organizations grounded in social consciousness requires ensuring that business decisions have the well-being of the people and the planet as core considerations. We need Impact Champions to advance socially-oriented innovations to make such organizations a reality.

Action Point 6: As an Impact Champion, You Must Initiate Corporate Social Innovations.

- Tap into your social consciousness even while making routine business decisions to not overlook when stakeholder or environmental well-being is being compromised.

- Self-identify yourself as the Impact Champion and take personal responsibility for initiating action.
- Find allies to support you in the cause and form coalitions to spread the word. Frame the message depending on your audience, highlighting moral versus pragmatic aspects.
- Create solution prototypes and test them. Accumulate small wins.
- Institutionalize the successful solutions within the organization or in the larger ecosystem by altering structures, policies, practices, and technology.

Social Entrepreneurship: Starting businesses for social impact

When you find it increasingly challenging to convince a corporate to initiate CSI and CSR to solve social and sustainability-related problems, it might be an opportune moment to move on in your journey as an Impact Champion—to a role that is external to your company.

Social Entrepreneurial Journey

✓ *Getting started—founder background and inspiration*
✓ *Finding co-founders and implementation partners*
✓ *Choosing a legal structure*
✓ *Developing a technology and business model*
✓ *Co-creating an ecosystem*

Action Point 7: As an Aspiring Impact Champion Keen to Address Wicked Problems, Social Entrepreneurship Offers an Opportunity to Fill the Institutional Voids Left Behind by the Public and Private Sectors

- As a Social Entrepreneur, you will be driven by your social consciousness, determined to make a social impact, and enthused by opportunities to create social value.
- A social enterprise offers a framework through which you can accomplish your vision.
- Build a local ecosystem to support your enterprise.
- Start by establishing relationships with various stakeholders, selling your ideas, spreading awareness, and garnering people to be part of your change efforts.
- Focus on evolving your Social Enterprise Business canvas.
- What is the value proposition and the unique contribution that your enterprise aims to deliver?
- How do you plan to create value? Your solutions can be focused on either technology or a business model innovation to solve societal challenges.
- How will you capture value? Since you are set with the avowed purpose of bringing social and environmental returns to their beneficiaries rather than making a profit for yourself, you will continually walk the tightrope, balancing social

outcomes for beneficiaries and earnings for your sustenance, scale, and growth.
- Pay attention to striking the right balance between social and financial value capture.

Getting a social enterprise off the ground: Understanding the funding and incubation landscape

Once you decide to step outside the boundaries of an organization to set up your enterprise, you will have to garner resources from the external business ecosystem independently. This can be a very daunting task for an aspiring social entrepreneur. We help you with information on the funding and incubation landscape, which will help you make the most appropriate choice and the best use of what is available.

Action Point 8: Choose the Most Appropriate Funding Options from the Array Available. Appreciate the Role of Impact Investors in Supporting Social Enterprises. Be Conversant with the Incubation Landscape

Funding sources:

- Begin with bootstrapping for an early-stage social venture. It helps the entrepreneur retain control over the business and is not bogged down by interest burden.

- The next recourse is friends and family—an extension of bootstrapping. It can be in the form of a gift, a loan, or equity. This source indicates the funder's faith in the founder and the idea, independent of market indicators.
- Research and development grants are ideal funding sources at the ideation and prototyping stage.
- Business plan competitions, social enterprise challenges, and case competitions are excellent avenues for small initial funding until the enterprise is ready for more significant investments.
- Crowdfunding is a popular option to test out early-stage projects and gain visibility by introducing a new idea to the market.
- Angels investors offer funds when a social enterprise still needs to build organizational processes and capabilities to reach the market.
- Venture fund investments come in later with a sizeable pot of money to further innovations and create profound social impact.
- Debt funds offer term loans that must be serviced in full along with interest and should be accessed only when the revenue stream is in place.

Impact Investors:

- Invest in social ventures that are likely to have a positive impact and environmental sustainability.

- Their focus areas are sustainable agriculture, clean energy, environmental conservation, healthcare, water and sanitation, affordable housing, skilling, and livelihood expansion programs.
- They expect lower returns from their investment in social ventures.
- They help through a range of asset classes—cash to fixed income, venture capital, and private equity.

Measuring social impact:

Social entrepreneurs must measure social impact as their core intentionality is to bring about a positive impact. Impact measurement involves the following steps:

- Set and state social and environmental objectives and share them with relevant stakeholders.
- Develop performance metrics/targets related to these objectives.
- Periodically monitor and manage the performance of investees against these targets.
- Report performance on social and environmental goals to stakeholders.

Incubation landscape:

- Incubators and accelerators are essential components of the startup ecosystem.
- By offering mentoring and network access, incubators become a go-to destination for fledgling enterprises.

- Early-stage startups are likely to benefit the most from their support. Startups that already have a set business plan and product need mentorship and help to scale up.
- Incubators offer a host of facilities, including guest lectures by established entrepreneurs, policymakers, and investors to whom pitches can be made.
- Accelerators work with enterprises ready with a minimum viable product (MVP stage) and facilitate the next growth spurt.
- Incubators and accelerators undertake a multi-stage selection process to select the social startup they are prepared to support. Their criteria include problem and beneficiary characteristics, type of impact, scalability, firm stage, financial sustainability, and the entrepreneur's vision and leadership capabilities.
- Most impact investors use in-house tools to track the impact, though global tools like IRIS are popular.
- Finally, remember that your social enterprise has to be profitable enough to self-sustain, though not essentially earn high returns.

My Promise to Nature

Invocation

I bow to our Mother Earth, beholder of us all,
For nurturing and sustaining our very existence.
I bow to the harbinger of hope as rain, water,
and snow
For the gulp that quenches and food that fills.

I bow to the blowing wind.
For oxygen—the beginning and the end of life.
I bow to the trees, small and tall
For their offer of food, clothing, and shelter.

I bow to the treasures buried deep, the minerals,
metals, and the energy
For they enrich, fortify, and strengthen us.
I bow to the mighty Sun.
For the light and warmth that keeps all alive.

Apology

I seek forgiveness
For ravaging the soil with chemicals, harsh and deadly
For piling up garbage, mounts and miles
In return for generous bounties.

I seek forgiveness
For poisoning every river, lake, and pond
With waste, refuse, and blackwater
In return for the purest drink and sustenance.

I seek forgiveness
For filling the air with noxious fumes, dust,
and smoke
From our factories, motors, and mindless festivities
That burst and burn in the name of gaiety.

I seek forgiveness
For cutting and logging many forests and a
million trees
Uprooting them from their very lands,
In return for their sheltering shade and water held for
us by their roots.

I seek forgiveness
For drilling, blasting, and overextracting,
Leaving the rich coffers depleted and empty
For the barrenness, we created where once gems
gleamed.

Pledge

I promise
To be conscious, considerate, and creative
To conserve what is left, to give back more than
what I take
To purify before I let go, to plant many more than
I pluck

This I shall do
By living simply, leaving behind enough for our little
ones to live
By caring deeply, nurturing Nature
By treating our waste, segregating it carefully
By using less, reusing, and upcycling
By maintaining biodiversity, protecting the massive
whale to the tiny worm
By recreating ways of living in harmony with
ourselves and all
By sharing the earth's abundance equally with
our brethren,
The marginalized, dispossessed, and the voiceless.

For we are all fragile threads of a spider's silk,
intertwined and interdependent
This, I shall remember, and the promise I shall keep!

**

An Impact Champion is:
Conscious of production and consumption
Considerate in usage—wastes minimum,
conserves maximum
Creative in finding new ways of doing the above.

Acknowledgments

Conversations with and insights from several people have shaped the ideas shared in this book. Heartfelt gratitude to Latha Poonamallee (New School & In Med Prognostics), Joanne Scillitoe (California State University), Sumelika Bhattacharyya (Goa Institute of Management), Nagaraja Prakasham (Angel Investor), Seema Prem (FIA Technology Services), Sameer Sawarkar (Neurosynaptic Communications), Siva Devireddy (Go Coop), Manoj Kumar (Social Alpha), Sarah Alexander (SELCO Foundation), Suresh Krishna (Yunus Social Business), Amit Antony Alex (Upaya), Mahesh Yagnaraman (Acumen), Arvind Agarwal (C4D), Srinivas Ramanujam (Villgro), Sivarajah Ramanathan (Nativelead), Jaya Umadikar (RTBI), Srikrishna Sridhar Murthy (Sattva Consulting), Manish Kothari (Rhino Machines), Priyanka Bapna (Meemansa), Meera Rajeevan (S.D. Foundation), Joseph Nixon (SBI Foundation), Jijo John (Calpine),

Suresh Kalagnanam (University of Saskatchewan), Sapna Poti (PSA's office-GoI), Joseph Sebastian (Faisal and Shabana Foundation).

List of Organizations and Corporations

1. Actionaid https://www.actionaidindia.org/
2. Acumen https://acumen.org/
3. Ameliorate Biotech https://amelioratebiotech.com/about/
4. Amity Innovation Incubators https://www.amity.edu/aii/
5. Amrita TBI https://www.amritatbi.com/
6. Aravind Eye Hospital https://aravind.org/
7. Asian Development Bank https://www.adb.org/
8. Atal Innovation Mission https://aim.gov.in/
9. Avishkar https://www.avishkarngo.org/
10. Bare Necessities https://barenecessities.in/
11. Bill and Melinda Gates Foundation https://www.gatesfoundation.org/
12. BITS Pilani https://www.bits-pilani.ac.in/
13. British Standards Institution https://www.bsigroup.com/en-IN/
14. BSR https://www.bsr.org/en/
15. Caspian https://www.caspian.in/
16. CETP https://www.mpcb.gov.in/waste-management/common-effluent-treatment-plant
17. Climate launchpad https://climatelaunchpad.org/
18. CultYvate https://yourstory.com/companies/cultyvate/amp
19. Department of Electronics and Information Technology https://www.meity.gov.in/
20. Dr. Reddy's https://www.drreddys.com/
21. Ecoparadigm https://www.ecoparadigm.com/
22. Ellen MacArthur Foundation https://www.ellenmacarthur foundation.org/news

23. Essel Propack https://www.eplglobal.com/
24. Eximius https://www.eximiusdesign.com/about-eximius/
25. FIA Technologies https://fiaglobal.com/
26. Global Impact Investing Network https://thegiin.org/
27. Godrej & Boyce https://www.godrej.com/godrejandboyce/
28. Hindustan Zinc Limited https://www.hzlindia.com/
29. IIIT Allahabad https://www.iiita.ac.in/
30. IIM Ahmedabad https://www.iima.ac.in/
31. IIM Calcutta https://www.iimcal.ac.in/
32. IIT Bombay https://www.iitb.ac.in/
33. IIT Delhi https://home.iitd.ac.in/
34. IIT Kharagpur http://www.iitkgp.ac.in/
35. Impact Investors Council https://iiic.in/
36. IndiaGoesGlobal https://indiagoesglobal.com/
37. Indian Angel Network https://www.indianangelnetwork.com/
38. Indian Hotels Company https://www.ihcltata.com/
39. Innaumation Medical Devices https://innaumation.com/
40. International Council for Local Environment Initiatives https://iclei-europe.org/who-we-are/#:~:text=ICLEI%20%E2%80%93%20Local%20Governments%20for%20Sustainability,governments%20committed%20to%20sustainable%20development
41. International Organization for Standardisation https://www.iso.org/home.html
42. ISRO https://www.isro.gov.in/
43. ITC https://www.itcportal.com/
44. JSW Group https://www.jsw.in/
45. Kamal Kisan https://www.kamalkisan.com/
46. LABS https://www.drreddys.com/OurCitizenship/SustainabilityReports/2013/livelihoods.asp
47. Lok Capital http://www.lokcapital.com/
48. Mahindra & Mahindra https://www.mahindra.com/
49. Meemansa https://www.meemansa.in/
50. Meghshala http://meghshala.online/
51. Michael and Susan Dell Foundation https://www.dell.org/
52. Ministry of Health and Family Welfare https://mohfw.gov.in/
53. Ministry of Housing and Urban Affairs http://mohua.gov.in/
54. Mirakle Couriers https://www.miraklecouriers.com/
55. Murugappa Group https://www.murugappa.com/
56. NASSCOM https://nasscom.in/

57. National Innovation Council https://www.india.gov.in/website-national-innovation-council
58. National Mission for Clean Ganga https://nmcg.nic.in/
59. National Skill Development Council https://nsdcindia.org/
60. Neurosynaptic https://www.neurosynaptic.com/
61. NITI Ayog http://niti.gov.in/
62. NIT Trichy https://www.nitt.edu/
63. OECD Forum https://www.oecd.org/forum/
64. Omidyar Network https://omidyar.com/
65. Oxfam International https://www.oxfam.org/en
66. Platform for Accelerating the Circular Economy https://pacecircular.org/
67. Power Finance Corporation Limited https://www.pfcindia.com/
68. Rajasthan Urban Improvement Trust https://urban.rajasthan.gov.in/content/raj/udh/uit-udaipur/en/home.html.html
69. Rhino Machines https://www.rhinomachines.net/
70. Rural Technology and Business Incubator http://www.rtbi.in/
71. SCOPE https://www.scope-india.in/
72. SELCO https://www.selcofoundation.org/
73. Small Industries Development Bank of India https://www.sidbi.in/
74. Social Alpha https://www.socialalpha.org/
75. SP Jain https://www.spjain.org/
76. SP Robotics https://sproboticworks.com/
77. State Bank of India https://www.onlinesbi.com/
78. Tata Group https://www.tata.com/
79. The Aditya Birla Group https://www.adityabirla.com/
80. Udaipur Municipal Corporation http://www.udaipurmc.org/HomePage.aspx
81. United Nations Environment Program https://www.unep.org/
82. Unitus Capital http://unituscapital.com/
83. Unlimited India https://unltdindia.org/
84. Upaya Social Ventures https://www.upayasv.org/
85. UN Women https://www.unwomen.org/en
86. US Aid https://www.usaid.gov/
87. Victory Art Foundation http://www.victoryartsfoundation.org/
88. Villgro https://villgro.org/
89. World Bank https://www.worldbank.org/en/home
90. World Economic Forum https://www.weforum.org/
91. Zoho https://www.zohocorp.com/
92. Zone startup https://india.zonestartups.com/
93. Venture Intelligence https://www.ventureintelligence.com/